"Stephen Miller has crafted an incredibly helpful book for anyone longing to break out of the bondage of sin and doubt and be liberated to walk by faith into a life that is much bigger than they could have imagined."

Paul Baloche, worship pastor and songwriter
of "Open the Eyes of My Heart"
and "Your Name"

"*Liberating King* is an encouraging contemplation of how the gospel overcomes our sin by showing us all that Jesus is and does for us. Christians will be encouraged by this book to further pursue Christ in the hope of glory."

Russell Moore, president, Southern Baptist
Ethics & Religious Liberty Commission

"Stephen Miller is a worshiper. Not a detached-from-real-life worshiper, but a man who integrates the 'nasty now and now' with the beauty of God's future. In *Liberating King*, he leads us on a journey to encounter a God who brings freedom to ordinary people just like us."

Darrin Patrick, lead pastor of The Journey St. Louis;
vice president of Acts 29;
chaplain to the St. Louis Cardinals

"Stephen Miller is a worship leader who cares deeply about the church, and this is evident through his music and writing. I'm grateful for the care he takes to connect gospel truths to real struggles everyone can relate to."

Matt Carter, pastor of preaching & vision,
Austin Stone Community Church

LIBERATING

KING

BREAKING FREE
FROM THE TYRANNY OF SIN

STEPHEN MILLER

BakerBooks

a division of Baker Publishing Group
Grand Rapids, Michigan

Published by Baker Books
a division of Baker Publishing Group
P.O. Box 6287, Grand Rapids, MI 49516-6287
www.bakerbooks.com

Printed in the United States of America

Library of Congress Cataloging-in-Publication Data is on file at the Library of Congress, Washington, DC.

ISBN 978-0-8010-0683-8

The author is represented by the literary agency of Wolgemuth & Associates, Inc.

16 17 18 19 20 21 22   7 6 5 4 3 2 1

To my wife, Amanda,
and our five kids, Kinsey, Keira, Jude, Liam, and Ethan.
May our eyes always stay fixed on Jesus
as we walk together with him.

———————

In memory of Ronnie Smith,
the impact of whose life
will ripple into eternity.

Contents

Contents

Acknowledgments

To my wife, Amanda. Thank you for your support, encouragement, and patience that helped me finish this, and for always pointing me to Jesus.

To my kids, Kinsey, Keira, Jude, Liam, and Ethan. You each inspire me and bring so much joy to my life.

To my parents, Ann Goodner and Lee Miller. Thank you for giving me life and supporting all my crazy ideas over the years.

To my other parents, Charles and Sonii Nagel. Thank you for taking me in like I was your own and giving me your daughter.

To my band, Taylor Webb, Ryan Rich, and Mason Terry. Thank you for the countless hours you have spent with me on the road and at our home church, selflessly serving others to bring glory to Jesus. And thank you for the months of driving me everywhere so that I could finish this book.

To Charlie Harrisberger, Matt Carter, Neil McClendon, Jim Frith, Tom Mosley, Darrin Patrick, J. R. Vassar, Bob

Kauflin, and Paul Baloche. I cannot tell you how much your mentorship over the years continues to shape me as a man and minister.

To my leadership team at Rooted Network—Glenn Packiam, Courtney Peebles, Lauren Chandler, and Andi Rozier. I am so grateful for your passion to equip and encourage worship leaders.

To Matt Boswell, Michael Bleecker, Mike Cosper, Aaron Ivey, Robbie Seay, Charlie Hall, Matt Papa, and Zac Hicks. Your friendship has been such an ongoing encouragement to me to keep growing deeper in my understanding of worship and love for Christ, his Word, and his church.

To Matt and Sara Harms. Thank you for letting me tell the story of you and Ava. Your faith has been such an inspiration to me and your lives have led me in worship so well over the last few years.

To Anita Smith. Thank you for your deep love for Jesus and for letting me tell the story of you and Ronnie. I can't think of a higher honor. Amanda and I have been deeply impacted by you both, and I can't wait until we get to celebrate together in heaven.

To my agent, Erik Wolgemuth. Thank you so much for helping me take this book from concept to completion and for believing in it so much!

To my editor, Brian Thomasson. Thank you for the hours spent helping me refine this and making it better than it would have been on my own.

To the amazing people at Baker Publishing. Thank you for investing in this book, that by God's grace he might use it to set many free with the liberating power of Christ.

Introduction

WHEN I RUN INTO A PROBLEM, I want to know the steps I need to take in order to pull myself up by my bootstraps and fix whatever is wrong. I love to think that ultimately I fixed the problem. I overcame by my strength and ingenuity. I earned whatever reward resulted.

Maybe you can relate to that.

The problem with this line of thinking is that it is completely false. You and I can't fix ourselves. In fact, we are probably the reason the problem exists in the first place. We were never designed to be our own savior, and trying to be will only drive us farther into the pit of despair. Like standing in quicksand—the harder we try to escape, the deeper we sink.

This book, despite its promise of helping you break free from the tyranny of sin, is not a self-help guide. I will not be telling you all the answers or giving you the twelve easy steps to a better you.

I am going to be very vulnerable with you. There is no sense in acting like I have it all together. I don't. I don't have the answers. In fact, I wrote every word on the pages that follow as a reminder to myself.

Despite being liberated from the power of sin, I find myself time and again running back to it. Just like Lot's wife, looking back toward Sodom. Like the Israelites constantly grumbling that they were better off staying in Egypt. I am a man who walks the high wire of faithfulness, and I'm not very good at it. In fact, I'm terrible. Falling off, repenting, getting back up. Falling off, repenting, getting back up. Falling off, repenting, getting back up. Rinse, repeat.

It's all quite discouraging sometimes. As I walk in this world, I am constantly bombarded with lies. I start to question who God has said I am and what he has told me to do. I was made to be a worshiper of God, but sin has so distorted the direction of my affection that my worship sometimes looks like a drunk driver being asked to walk the line for a sobriety test. I want to walk straight, to worship the one true God, but I keep turning to the right and the left and stumbling over my own feet.

Jesus says that he is the Truth, his Word is truth, that the Spirit of Truth lives in me, and that the truth sets me free. But sometimes I don't feel very free. I feel more like I'm in bondage. I feel broken.

It was from that place of brokenness, overwhelmed with discouragement at how slowly my sanctification seemed to be going, that I began to cry out for God to rescue me. I was following Jesus, but in the midst of an incredibly difficult season of life, I seemed to be losing the battle with doubt and pride.

That summer, I was leading worship at a student event in Santa Fe, surrounded by mountains on every side. I decided to take an afternoon of solitude. In hindsight it might not have been the best idea to go for a hike into the wilderness all by myself, but I climbed to the top of the highest peak I could see and began to cry out to God.

As I looked out over mile after mile of breathtaking majesty, it began to sink in that Jesus was using this difficult time to set me free. That all this struggle and strife was his gift to help me see the truth that he was there with me all along, a Liberating King at work on my heart, committed to delivering me from my bondage.

And there from that mountain, the words that would become my song "Liberating King" began to flow from my lips:

> There is no other in heaven and earth
> Who's strong enough to save
> No other God or King would ever lay his own life
>   down
> There's no one higher
> The one who bowed low has taken up his crown
> Our Liberating King, the one to set us free has
>   come.[1]

Jesus is here. He is with us. He is for us. He is in us. He is our only hope. Because Christ has come, made himself low, died in our place, and defeated sin and death, we *can* be free.

This book is for broken people like me. People who need a hope that is bigger than self-help. People who need a Savior who is stronger than themselves. People who need to stop believing the lies that surround them and start believing the truth.

If you're perfect, then you really don't need to keep reading. But if you, like me, find yourself day after day in need of a Savior to liberate you, then read on.

What I'm going to say here isn't really original. It comes from God's Word. I'm simply going to point to that light and let him expose the lies of our culture that seek to enslave us and illuminate the truth that sets us free.

I trust that his voice is loud enough to cut through all the noise.

1

Encountering the Truth

HOW THE LIBERATING KING FREES US FROM THE BONDAGE OF LIES

If you abide in my word, you are truly my disciples, and you will know the truth, and the truth will set you free. . . . Truly, truly, I say to you, everyone who practices sin is a slave to sin. The slave does not remain in the house forever; the son remains forever. So if the Son sets you free, you will be free indeed.

John 8:31–36

Jesus said to him, "I am the way, and the truth, and the life. No one comes to the Father except through me."

John 14:6

Now the Lord is the Spirit, and where the Spirit of the Lord is, there is freedom.

2 Corinthians 3:17

A FEW YEARS BACK I was invited to lead worship for a church's weekend services and gladly accepted, but I had no idea what I was getting myself into. On the whole the church was fantastic—incredibly welcoming and friendly, with an obvious love for Jesus and passion for worshiping him.

As we began to sing songs of praise and adoration, I couldn't help but notice a woman on the right side of the room, practicing what looked to be some sort of pantomimed samurai ninja sword fighting. It became very hard to focus on what I was there to do, and it seemed that the people I was trying to lead were having a difficult time with the distraction as well. Everyone had all but stopped singing and was staring at this woman, who seemed to be intensely engaged in the heat of some sort of imaginary battle.

When the service ended, I walked over to her as quickly as I could, curious to see what her actions were all about.

Beaming with pride and speaking with a thick southern accent, she said, "This room is at war, and I was in spiritual battle with the evil spirits over the souls of all these people. Pretty sure we won."

I had no words. I just stood there with what had to look like a bewildered, sheepish grin on my face.

That moment goes down in my book as one of the top three weirdest things I have experienced in church. And yet there is some truth there. There is a war raging all around us, and one of its most effective weapons is distraction.

Have you ever been in a room desperately trying to focus on the conversation you're having with the person right in front of you but instead finding yourself distracted by all the sights and sounds around you? It's hard to pay attention to what really matters because so much noise is drowning it out. It can be incredibly frustrating.

But isn't that the world we live in? It seems we can scarcely go one hour without the world whispering into our ears, appealing to our sin-sick hearts and distracting us from what really matters.

Advertisements and billboards fill our sight lines while radio commercials fill our ears. Television shows and music tell us what we need to have and who we need to be.

The grocery store checkout aisle bombards us with magazine covers that show us how we should look, what kind of sex we should be having and how often we should be having it, what kind of vacations we should take, what our homes should look like, and what food should be served in those homes.

Social media reminds us that despite our best efforts, we aren't successful enough, fit enough, or crafty enough; our lives are not "share-able," "retweet-able," or "pin-able" enough. We don't quite measure up to how things "should" be.

Little by little, day after day, these subtle and not-so-subtle messages creep into our hearts. They shape the way we see the world. They captivate our thinking.

If I only had _____, I would be happy—and I deserve to be happy.

If I only made more money, I wouldn't have to worry so much.

If only my spouse understood me (or, if only I were married), I wouldn't struggle with loneliness.

If I could just get that job or promotion, I would be fulfilled.

But these are all lies that were expertly engineered to enslave you and me, deftly designed for our destruction. Let's take a step back for a moment and logically examine how absurd these lies are.

> If having that "thing" is the *only* thing that will make us happy, then not having it will only make us miserable.
>
> If getting the promotion is the *only* way we can truly be fulfilled, then not getting it means we are doomed to frustrated discontent.

If only we could look beyond the flowery marketing of consumerism, peel back the facade of idolatry, and see the effect of these hollow promises and false hopes on our hearts.

You and I weren't made for these kinds of subpar desires and dreams, and we certainly weren't remade for them. This is not how things are supposed to be.

Yet this is the room we're sitting in, desperately trying to focus on the God right in front of us who is promising us freedom and satisfaction while we are distracted by the sparkling allure of the world's false promises that ultimately lead to bondage and discontent. How do we choose wisely and walk in the promise of freedom that has been offered to us in Christ? How do we fight for our own joy and satisfaction?

The truth is, knowing how illogical and unhelpful something is will not keep us from choosing it over and over again.

Knowing that porn will only bring emptiness and guilt will not keep the porn addict from choosing to stare at a screen night after night. Knowing that the hyper-photoshopped cover model is impossible to emulate will not keep a woman from choosing to go deeply into debt buying clothes, makeup, surgeries, personal trainers, and more. She needs a vision of something more beautiful and lovely.

We all do.

Our gaze must be fixed on something better and more excellent, something that will never be found lacking. This is why Paul tells us in Philippians 4:8 that if we want the true peace that comes with freedom in Christ, we should think on whatever is excellent, noble, just, lovely, pure, and honorable. He is commending us to be set free from the anxiety of trusting in things and people by trusting in the one who made everything and rules over all!

There is a difference between logic and truth. Logic speaks to your intellect. Truth speaks to your soul. Solid logic may free you up in many ways, but it will never be powerful enough to set you free. Only truth can do that. In worship, you interact with the truth in the most practical, life-changing way possible.

I have had the immeasurable joy of leading worship in the church for sixteen years now. There are few things that bring me more delight than getting to lead the people of God to sing the praises of God in the presence of God. In fact, it is so fulfilling to me that it's difficult to think in terms of worship without thinking of music and singing. Certainly worship is much more than songs, and I could likely fill an entire book talking about what worship is and isn't. But for the sake of clarity, I will define worship here as "our entire life's response to God's character and actions."

You and I are always worshiping—when our church gathers to sing and when our family gathers around the dinner table. When we are driving down the freeway, working hard at our jobs, or caring for the poor, we are worshiping.

Nonetheless, I believe some forms of worship lead to a more intentional lifestyle of worship. The form of worship I will focus on in this book is the intentional discipline of silencing the competing voices all around us in order to ground our hearts in Christ's freedom by rehearsing the truth of God's Word, being filled with the truth by God's Spirit, and encountering the Truth himself (Jesus).

Rehearsing the Truth

I've learned that there's a profound difference between knowing something with my head and knowing it with my heart.

I am the king of multitasking. I can be talking to my wife while watching a show on television, texting on my phone, checking Twitter on my iPad, and keeping up with the game on my laptop. At the end of the night, I could probably give you a general rundown of all that went on, but did I truly experience any of it? No! I passively let a bunch of information happen to me, rather than actively participating in a meaningful way.

Similarly, worship is not passively going through the motions of quickly thinking good, logical thoughts about God. It is rehearsing the truth of God's Word; actively meditating on it and letting it sink into and shape the innermost core of our being—our hearts. It is replacing all the messages of the world with the good news of who God is, what he has done, and who we are in light of that.

This discipline naturally forces the direction of our gaze Godward and changes the way we see the world in light of his glory. Our meditations shape our motivations.

All of a sudden, even the most mundane of tasks has new meaning.

All of a sudden, nothing is ever quite as bad as it seems.

Think about it. If you know in your heart that God is perfect, all his ways are perfect, and every good and perfect gift comes from him, then when he tells you something, you can trust that it is true and right and just. He will not deceive you. All he has told you and me is for our good, and there is no area of our lives where God's goodness is removed.

When someone else gets the recognition we long for and we're tempted to give in to the sin of envy and comparison, we can worship, saying, "God is good and he does good. He has me where I am right now for a reason, and I can trust him when he gives and when he takes away."

As we worship, we remember that God is completely sovereign, completely powerful, and completely in control. Nothing in this world can happen apart from his will. Nothing catches him off guard, slips through his fingers, or forces his hand.

So when our world is spinning out of control and we are tempted to try to control everything or weep with desperation, we can worship, saying, "God is powerful and sovereign. He is in control right now, so I don't have to be. I can trust him."

As we worship, we remember that God is love and he is loving. In fact, the truest word for love is *Jesus*. He is the most perfect, purest demonstration of love in all of history. His steadfast love will endure forever. It will never fail us and it will never bail on us.

So when we feel rejected or unloved and are tempted to numb the pain with food, porn, alcohol, and more, or when we feel the need to project an inflated, more lovable image to the world, instead we can worship. We can say, "God has created me in his image, purchased me with his blood, and adopted me into his family. I have value and worth because I am loved by God."

Jesus teaches us to approach God in worship not as outsiders but as adopted children of a loving Father (Matt. 6:9). The implications of this great truth are impossible to exaggerate.

If God is good, sovereign, loving, and he's my Father, then I have no need to worry. I have no need to envy, compare, be anxious, or be in control. I have no need to look to sin to give me hope, satisfaction, worth, or value. I have all I need in Christ, who is my life.

As we worship God, we are rehearsing the great, unshakable truths of God's Word, and the power of sin begins to lose its grip on our lives. The power of a newer, greater affection replaces the old ones that once held us in captivity, and we are set free.

Filled with the Truth

When I speak of meditation, it's important to understand exactly what I'm talking about. I don't mean the Eastern mysticism practice of emptying our minds. On the contrary, I mean the exact opposite. When we worship, we are not only emptying our minds of what is false, we are also filling our minds with the excellent majesty and glory of God's truth.

Yet if I were to tell you that the way out of bondage to sin is simply to "think happy thoughts," you would look at me like I was crazy. This isn't Neverland. There is no magic pixie dust to help us fly away from our problems if we just think happy thoughts.

I can't think of a more hopelessly cruel thing than to tell you that if you want to be liberated from sin, you just need to accumulate true thoughts that you can intellectually process for long periods of time.

There must be more to what's prescribed in the Scriptures as the way to relentlessly put to death all of our sinful desires.

We must be filled with the Spirit.

To empty ourselves of all that would keep us in bondage, we must offer up our whole lives to be filled with the liberating power of God's Spirit, the person of God whose very presence brings us freedom (2 Cor. 3:17).

When we worship, we are somehow mysteriously filled with the truth in the presence of the Holy Spirit. He is the Spirit of Truth who guides us in truth and shows us what is true about God and ourselves.

Worship invites the Spirit to engage the projector of our imaginations and display the glory of God in living color on the screen of our hearts. As we gaze upon the beauty and holiness of God in worship, we cannot help but see how unlike him we are. Our sins are brought to light by his voice of conviction, and we are compelled to dethrone all idols and exalt the one true God to his rightful place upon the throne of our hearts.

The Spirit that fills us illuminates the Scriptures to our hearts so that we can understand them, and he empowers us to live in obedience to them. He shows us what is true and what is not.

In the movie *Catch Me If You Can*, Leonardo DiCaprio plays a con man named Frank Abagnale, an expert at writing fraudulent checks. Frank mastered the art of forging checks so effectively that even the banks couldn't tell the difference between what was real and what was false. In the end, he was caught, and the FBI turned to Frank's expertise to help catch other forgers. Because Frank was keenly able to detect the truth and the lie, he was uniquely qualified to act as a counselor to help the FBI see the difference.

There is a master forger out there. He has been at the game a lot longer than we can imagine, and he has gotten really good at what he does. He is called the Father of Lies because he has so twisted the world we live in that the truth looks like the lie and the lie looks like the truth. He is constantly throwing counterfeit gods at us, enticing us with false hope that he expects will keep us in chains, and our hearts are so sick with sin that we have a hard time telling the difference.

But the Holy Spirit is an expert counselor who not only *shows* us the truth but also *fills* us with truth. When we worship, he opens the eyes of our hearts to see the hopelessly empty lies as well as the gloriously liberating truth of the gospel that we might be set free.

Encountering the Truth

I'm captivated by the story in Luke 8 about the man who had been tormented by demons for years. The seemingly indomitable power that possessed and oppressed him had him shackled to a state of desperate agony. But when the Truth showed up, the lie was made painfully obvious. When Jesus came on the scene, everything changed.

The demons who before had seemed so fierce and untamable all of a sudden start cowering like puppies with their tails between their legs, begging Jesus not to torment them the way they had tormented the man.

Talk about total dominance. This is what true power looks like. Jesus doesn't have to say or do anything. They know about him. He has a reputation. He is the King of all, who created all things and rules over all things. These demons are right to be afraid.

Jesus sets the man free from the oppression of the demons and gives him hope for a new life that he could have never dreamed of before.

This is the power of the presence of God. Even demons quake in their boots when he shows up. The captive is set free. The impossible becomes possible.

In the movie *Braveheart*, the Scottish people are led by William Wallace to fight for their freedom against the tyrannical reign of England. At one point, a squadron of English soldiers chases down a couple of Scottish scouts until their backs are up against the wall. Confidently the soldiers shout out, "You're outnumbered and trapped! Now where's Wallace?"

The situation looks dire. Any onlooker would advise them to give up.

Yet right when it seems things can't get uglier for the scouts, a rock comes flying from above, pegging the cocky soldier in the head. The camera pans up and there stands Wallace with a sly look on his face, waving, his band of soldiers surrounding him. There is no contest. Wallace's crew makes light work of the English, and they continue their fight for freedom.

This is what Jesus does for us. No matter how dire the situation looks, the truth remains that the cameras will soon pan up and our hero will be standing there, ready to save the day. His reputation precedes him as a dominating warrior triumphant over sin and death. He has won and he will win. End of story.

You and I are plagued by our own "demons," pursued by the enemy until our backs are up against a wall. We can feel tormented, shackled, and powerless.

Perhaps you're experiencing inescapable guilt from past failures, or debilitating condemnation over the habitual sins you struggle with even now. Maybe you have been sinned against and can't move on from bitterness into forgiveness. Maybe you can't stop comparing yourself to others, and as a result, you feel you will never be good enough to be used by God for anything significant.

These lies torment and enslave us. We need the Truth to show up and make everything right, to come on the scene and put all the lies to flight.

God has given us himself. This means that just as he is not a one-dimensional God, the freedom he gives is not one-dimensional freedom. It is an ever-increasing, ever-deepening, all-encompassing liberty that will help us not only finish strong but run the race of this life with joy and satisfaction.

He set us free so that the Spirit could produce the fruit of that freedom in our lives. We can love deeper, overflowing with profound happiness that isn't based on our circumstances but on his incomprehensible and ever-present peace and patience. We are free to impact the world around us with his supernatural kindness, goodness, faithfulness, gentleness, and self-control.

Jesus said, "I am the way, and the truth, and the life. No one comes to the Father except through me" (John 14:6).

This isn't some cute saying. It's foundational. When Jesus calls himself the Truth, he is saying, "I'm here to set you free from the bondage of lies." When he says, "I am the way," it means more than, "If you come with me, you'll get to go to heaven." Jesus is our way out and our way in! Out of bondage, into freedom. Not freedom to do whatever we want, but freedom to live a life worth living. It is a life with Christ at the center, as the Sun that our entire world revolves around with the light of his glory exposing all the shoddy counterfeits and inferior forgeries that would keep us trapped in darkness.

We see this best when we come to him in worship. In worship, as we rehearse the truth of God's Word and are filled with the truth by his Spirit, we are also encountering the Truth himself in the person of Jesus. He is our perfect High Priest and Mediator who takes us boldly before the throne of God, where he is seated with power in the heavens.

The great mystery of this is that God infinitely occupies all time and space. Heaven is his throne, the earth his footstool. There is nowhere we can go to escape from him. And yet as we ground our worship fully in the truth of God's Word, by the power of the Holy Spirit, Jesus chooses to meet with us in a unique way and take us into the presence of the Father.

No lie can stand in his presence and not be seen for what it is. No chain can remain on us when our eyes are fixed intently on the Liberating King in worship. When Jesus—the Truth himself—shows up, everything changes.

We are set free.

27

Questions for Application and Discussion

1. What are some of the lies that you believe about God, yourself, and the world? What does God's unchanging word of truth have to say about it? Open a Bible right now and begin to remind yourself of what is true.

2. What are the areas of ongoing struggle in your life? Where do you need to be set free? How could worshiping the Liberating King set you free in these specific areas?

3. What can you intentionally do to silence the noise of your life and consistently get alone in order to rehearse the truth, actively be filled with truth, and encounter the Truth? What times of day work best? Make a plan. Schedule it as you would your workout, mealtime, or meetings.

2

When Sorrows like Sea Billows Roll

HOW THE LIBERATING KING
FREES US TO SUFFER WELL

The crowd joined in attacking them. . . . They threw them into prison, ordering the jailer to keep them safely. . . . About midnight Paul and Silas were praying and singing hymns to God, and the prisoners were listening to them, and suddenly there was a great earthquake, so that the foundations of the prison were shaken. And immediately all the doors were opened, and everyone's bonds were unfastened. When the jailer woke and saw that the prison doors were open, he drew his sword and was about to kill himself, supposing that the prisoners had escaped. But Paul cried with a loud voice, "Do not harm yourself, for we are all here." And the jailer called for lights and rushed in, and trembling with fear he fell down before Paul and Silas. Then he brought them out and said, "Sirs, what must I do to be saved?" And they said, "Believe in the Lord Jesus, and you will be saved, you and your household."

Acts 16:22–23, 25–31

FULL DISCLOSURE: I have done some jail time.

When I was a kindergartner, I had a stealing problem. If I saw change on my dad's dresser, I would take it so that I could buy gum from the gas station. I thought that it was such a small amount that my dad would never notice, but I was definitely wrong about that.

One afternoon he confronted me and told me that I was going to jail for stealing. That's where thieves end up. We got in the car, he took me to the local jailhouse, and the officer locked me up.

I was devastated. I was too young to go to prison. I had such a bright future ahead of me.

Yet there I stood in the cell for what seemed like an eternity before the officer finally came in, told me not to steal anymore, and let me go.

Looking back, my experience was more humorous than anything. The jail cell was pretty sterile, the officer very cordial. There were no other prisoners foaming at the mouth, looking through the cell bars with murderous glares in their eyes. I was never assaulted or chained up. It was about as far as you can get from what Paul and Silas were facing in Philippi in Acts 16.

As a kid, when I would read about Paul and Silas being thrown into jail, I imagined an American kindergartner's unfortunate "let's teach him a lesson" environment. But ancient

Philippian prisons were designed to immediately obliterate any daydreams of escape, to crush any and all hope of freedom. In stark contrast to the relatively comfortable, humane settings of modern Western prisons, the prisons in Philippi were more like dungeons—underground caves carved out of the rock.

It was there in a damp, cold hole in the ground that Paul and Silas's bloody, mangled bodies were shackled with iron stocks and chains and guarded by ruthless, sword-wielding Roman soldiers. There was not even a glimmer of hope to escape unless God came through.

Yet there they sat in shackles, not shaken by their suffering but singing in the midst of it. Not songs of "Woe is me!" but songs of *worship* to their one true King.

This kind of uncommon reaction catches my modern American evangelical sensibilities off guard. I tend to like my Christianity to be pretty comfortable—or at least not uncomfortable. I hate suffering. If I'm stuck behind a slow driver in the fast lane for too long, I start grumbling. Don't get me started on being stuck in a seemingly hopeless situation that I have no control over.

Yet the idea of comfortable Christianity was as foreign to the first-century church as the idea of Snapchat is to a modern-day octogenarian. Suffering came with the territory. When Jesus told his followers, "Take up your cross and follow me," they did it, some of them literally. The apostles and disciples were beaten, whipped, stoned, imprisoned, exiled, beheaded, and even crucified.

Throughout history, martyrs were tied to posts and burned alive. Rather than recant their dedication to Christ, they would instead sing hymns of praise as the flames engulfed their bodies. Rather than weeping, cursing, or feverishly begging for their lives, they instead had a tranquility that came from knowing that someone greater than their suffering was present with them in the midst of it.

When you realize God is present, it doesn't matter if you're chained in a jail cell or walking to your death. Even in the darkest days—from losing your job to downsizing or your retirement savings to a market crash, from losing a child to a miscarriage or a spouse to cancer—the God of all comfort is with you, able to comfort you beyond all comprehension.

This is how worship sets us free to suffer well.

When we worship, whether through corporate singing or private prayer and studying the Scriptures, we encounter the Truth himself in the person of Jesus. As he fills us with the Spirit of Truth and the Word of Truth, we are being prepared for the battle of suffering.

God is with us. He is for us. He is in us. He will never leave nor forsake us. He is working all things together for the good of those who love him and are called according to his purposes (Rom. 8:28). He is sovereign and loving and big enough to use even our suffering to prepare "an eternal weight of glory" to which even the worst affliction can't compare (2 Cor. 4:17).

It's hard to see even the most monumental of problems as anything bigger than light and momentary when you are staring at the grandeur and supremacy of a God whose throne is heaven and whose footstool is earth. It's hard not to feel safe when you're worshiping at the feet of a Liberating King who formed the deepest depths and highest heights.

Horatio Spafford was a very successful lawyer and businessman in Chicago in the nineteenth century. He had a beautiful family and loved Jesus. However, after the Great

Chicago Fire of 1871 destroyed most of his real estate investments (along with his entire life savings), he was left financially devastated.

Over the next two years, Spafford's world spiraled downward and his family became desperately aware of the toll their suffering had taken on them. He planned a vacation to England with his wife, Anna, and their four daughters, but right before they were to leave, a business development kept him back in the States. He and Anna decided that she and the girls would go on ahead and he would join them in a few days.

His family boarded the French steamship, *Ville du Havre*, and departed for England. But along the way, the *Ville du Havre* collided with an iron sailing ship and sank within minutes. Many refer to this wreck as the worst collision at sea to date before the sinking of the *Titanic*.

The next day, Spafford got a telegram from Anna: she alone had survived—his four daughters had died along with 226 other passengers. It was there, in the depths of anguish and loss, as he sailed to meet his grieving wife, that he wrote the cherished words of the hymn "It Is Well with My Soul."

> When peace, like a river, attendeth my way,
> When sorrows like sea billows roll;
> Whatever my lot, Thou has taught me to say,
> It is well, it is well, with my soul.
>
> My sin, oh, the bliss of this glorious thought!
> My sin, not in part, but the whole,
> Is nailed to the cross, and I bear it no more,
> Praise the Lord, praise the Lord, O my soul!

And Lord, haste the day when my faith shall be sight,
The clouds be rolled back as a scroll;
The trump shall resound, and the Lord shall descend,
Even so, it is well with my soul.[1]

No matter what you are suffering, you can still have peace and still rejoice in the truth that Jesus paid the ultimate price to rescue you from the ultimate suffering of death, hell, and eternal separation from God.

No matter how low you are, Jesus went lower. No matter how you are suffering, Jesus suffered more. No matter how abandoned and betrayed you feel, he felt more abandoned and betrayed. As he bore your sin and death, not only did all his friends turn away from him—even the Father hid his face!

As the perfect, righteous Son, Jesus shared eternal, unbroken fellowship with his perfect, righteous Father. But when he who knew no sin became our sin so that we might become his righteousness (2 Cor. 5:21), the Father looked away and poured out his holy wrath on sin (Isaiah 53; Rom. 3:25; Mark 15:34). Jesus was forsaken that you and I might never be! And because of his perfect sacrifice—because of his perfect suffering—God raised him from the dead and gave him the name that is above every name, the name that alone has the power to save!

This is our Liberating King—the one who laid low Satan, sin, and death. Through his suffering, he conquered our greatest and final enemy, and he will one day return to put a decisive end to all suffering.

As you and I worship him in the midst of our unique situations, no matter how grave, we are encountering the very

Savior who conquered the grave! He endured every storm we might ever face so that he could carry us into and out of them all.

In worship, we draw near to him in a way that says, "This is too much for me right now and I'm weary, but you are my refuge and strength." In the midst of troubles and trials, we are telling our souls the truth—that God is still ruling and reigning, in control and able to help. In our deepest sorrow, worship is remembering what we know to be true—that God is using our suffering to shape us into the image of Christ. That somehow this is not happening *to* us but *for* us, because nothing can get to us without going through him first.

As I read the Psalms, I am struck by how often the writers reminded themselves of the character and ways of God when going through various struggles. Though they faced overwhelming sorrow, they would remind themselves of how God had always been faithful to come through before, and they would worship, singing:

> I waited patiently for the LORD;
>   he inclined to me and heard my cry.
> He drew me up from the pit of destruction,
>   out of the miry bog,
> and set my feet upon a rock,
>   making my steps secure.
> He put a new song in my mouth,
>   a song of praise to our God.
> Many will see and fear,
>   and put their trust in the LORD. (Ps. 40:1–3)

Another writer prays this pointed, but hope-filled prayer:

35

Why are you cast down, O my soul,
    and why are you in turmoil within me?
Hope in God; for I shall again praise him,
    my salvation and my God. (Ps. 42:5)

This is such an honest expression of worship. No gimmicks. No beating around the bush. No trying to fake that things really aren't as bad as they feel. Simply raw, unadulterated, childlike worship that says, "God, I'm in turmoil. I feel like everything is falling apart. But I know you will never fall apart, so I'm hoping in you and coming before you in worship." The psalmist is choosing to worship rather than grumble and complain. He is filling his mind, memory, and mouth with the truth that God is faithful, just, and true.

Matt and Sara are dear friends to my wife and me and easily the most godly, incredible couple I have ever known. In 2011, they welcomed a sweet baby girl into their beautiful family—a fourth daughter named Ava Gabrielle.

Due to complications with Sara's pregnancy, Ava was born at twenty-seven weeks, five days, weighing only two pounds, eleven ounces. She spent her first few months on earth in the NICU but seemed to be flourishing to the point that the doctors called her a show-off. She was growing stronger by the day, and things were looking up until one day when they noticed Ava's head was growing too quickly.

She was diagnosed with hydrocephalus, a blockage that keeps fluids from being distributed from within the brain, and surgeons had to operate on her brain twice. In the midst of all that, Ava also began to have back-to-back uncontrollable seizures that required high doses of medication to counteract.

She would sleep most of the day and lost her drive to eat and even breathe.

Matt is incredibly brilliant—a doctor himself. So, with the help of a pediatric neurologist friend, he began looking at Ava's MRIs, biopsies, labs, and genetic tests in order to try and discover what might actually be causing all of this.

The research and tests showed that Ava had an incredibly rare genetic disease called Alexander's disease, which causes cells in the brain to overgrow, over-divide, and crowd out the normal cells needed to think and move. It's a one-in-three-million disease, but thus far it has been uniformly fatal, with fifteen months being the longest a child with Alexander's disease has survived.

For months, Sara and Matt switched off shifts at the hospital. Some weeks Ava would come home and they were able to have a semi-normal life for a short period of time. But it was never long before they were back to the hospital. I would visit from time to time to bring a meal and pray with them. It's hard watching your friends go through something so painful and being powerless to help, with no answers to give.

The hospital room always felt so sacred—like holy ground, the presence of God was so tangible. Sara is a worship leader and with every visit, she had worship music playing as she held Ava, singing over her—leading her own soul to worship in the midst of all the suffering and uncertainty and leading *me* in worship as I struggled with why such an amazing family would be going through something like this. Sara reminded all of us of the truth of who God is—a good, loving Father who would somehow use this to make something beautiful.

One day things looked especially grim, so I went to the hospital to pray for God to heal Ava. Holding a helpless baby in my arms, knowing this might be her last week on earth, overwhelmed me to the point that I could barely get through my prayer. I just stood there weeping. Sara began to share a song with me that had been ministering to her, and she said, "Worshiping Jesus is the only way I am getting through this. I know he is with me. I know he is good. And worshiping is reminding me of that truth."

Just a few days later, on her first birthday, Ava found her ultimate healing. Sara asked me to sing "Great Is Thy Faithfulness" and "Never Once" at her memorial. What a profound request. She had just lost her baby, and she wanted to sing about God's great, unending faithfulness. So we did.

> Never once did we ever walk alone
> Never once did you leave us on our own
> You are faithful, God, You are faithful.[2]

Worship frees us to suffer well because someone greater than our suffering is in our midst. The one who has the final say on everything, who is faithful in all things, no matter what, is with us.

As you and I worship in the midst of our struggles, trials, and storms, Jesus Christ—the Truth himself—is interceding on our behalf before the Father and speaking the truth over us. The Spirit, our Comforter and Helper, is there inhabiting our praise, filling us with the truth that God is for us and that every trial we endure is for our good.

We can worship no matter what our circumstances because God's character is not circumstantial. No matter what we are walking through, he remains true. No matter how we are suffering, God remains faithful. No matter how dark it gets, no matter how grim, we are not hopeless. Our hope does not shift or shake, falter or fail because it is built on the Solid Rock, the unchanging one with whom there is no shadow of change. He completes all he begins.

There will be beauty from this.

One day, he will return and wipe away every tear and there will be no more suffering. One day, he will make all things right and all things new, and we will look back and see that none of our pain was wasted, none of our suffering was pointless. One day, we will worship and adore a God who truly did work together all things for the good of those who love him and were called according to his purpose.

Because we know that day is coming, we have total freedom to worship in the midst of this one.

Questions for Application and Discussion

1. In what way are you suffering now? How do you feel about it? Be honest with yourself and God. Try to avoid Band-Aid statements. It does no good to sugarcoat or pretend you're not hurting. Be real about how you're feeling. God is big enough to handle it. I promise.

2. What lies do you believe about your suffering, yourself, and God? How can you replace those lies with the truth of Scripture and worship God in the midst of your suffering?

3. In what way is God using your suffering to shape and sanctify you? Take a few moments to praise him for that.

3

Someone Greater
Than the Storm

And when he got into the boat, his disciples followed him. And behold, there arose a great storm on the sea, so that the boat was being swamped by the waves; but he was asleep. And they went and woke him, saying, "Save us, Lord; we are perishing." And he said to them, "Why are you afraid, O you of little faith?" Then he rose and rebuked the winds and the sea, and there was a great calm. And the men marveled, saying, "What sort of man is this, that even winds and sea obey him?"

Matthew 8:23–27

So why should I worry? Why do I freak out? God knows what I need. . . . Two things you told me. That you are strong and you love me. Your love is strong.

Jon Foreman

I STILL REMEMBER THE FIRST TIME I saw Zack Morris holding a cell phone. (If you don't know Zack Morris from *Saved by the Bell*, you're missing an important aspect of early '90s television history.) That thing looked like a thirty-pound beige brick with a pole sticking out of it, but it was so cool. Growing up, my family had one of those rotary dial telephones, so a portable, wireless phone was amazing to me.

Fast-forward two decades and phones run the world! You can take pictures, run your calendar, check your email, listen to music, and watch movies on your phone. Our phones have become our alarm clocks, wallets, Bibles, and more. Want to lose weight? There's an app for that. Want to know what that song was? There's an app for that. Want to speak face-to-face with someone on the other side of the planet? There's an app for that. Everywhere we go, we have the power of a virtually endless stream of information right at our fingertips in the form of a five-inch screen that fits in our pocket.

It is amazing what humans can do, and cell phones are just the beginning. We can successfully replace a failing human heart with another healthy human heart. We can fly through the air at hundreds of miles per hour. We can go to the moon, get out and walk around, and then come back. We can build robots to search the depths of the ocean or send them to seek out distant galaxies. We can split atoms and create weapons that can obliterate entire cities. We can clone animals.

Yet in spite of all the progress we have made, all the power that we wield, the reality is that there is still far more in this world that we are absolutely powerless to control. Earthquakes, floods, tsunamis, tornadoes, hurricanes, volcanoes, stock market crashes, disease, death. The old maxim "control is an illusion" may not be completely true, but it is pretty close. No matter how sophisticated our technology, no matter how much we work out, eat right, and take our vitamins—no matter how well we build the *Titanic*, if it hits the right iceberg, that thing is going down.

Think of the student who graduates college with a 4.0 GPA and is still forced to move back in with his parents because he can't find a job. Or the parents who spend time with their kids every day, training them in good behavior, only to have them go crazy as soon as they move away from home.

You can make all the right investments and still lose everything if a terrorist crashes a plane into a building. Or you can be the hardest worker in your company and still lose your job to downsizing.

This reminds me of the story of Jesus's disciples battling a storm in the boat (Mark 4:35–41). It didn't matter how skilled they were as fishermen or sailors, or how well built their boat was. They were worried out of their minds, powerless to control their own fate and convinced they were moments away from the end. In their anxiety, they turned to Jesus, fuming.

"Don't you *care* that we are going to *die*!?"

Jesus seemed completely unfazed by the reality that they were in a storm. He was resting peacefully, trusting by faith in a greater reality—that his Father would take care of them. The thought of worry or fear never entered his mind. In response to the panic of his disciples, he gets up and tells the storm to knock it off. The wind and waves immediately die down. In an instant, the disciples' worry turns to worship.

"Who is this that even the wind and waves obey him?"

Considering who was in the boat with them, it's baffling that the disciples got so worked up. However, if I'm honest, I find myself there in that boat freaking out with them more often than I would like to admit.

When we trust in anything other than Jesus, we are setting ourselves up for anxiety when the storms come—and they *will* come, sometimes with fury and ruthlessness. There will be days when the reckless wrath of unforgiving, unrelenting, uncaring waves will smash against us on all sides, threatening to capsize us, and we will be powerless to help ourselves. And in those moments, we must remember the truth that the Liberating King, the one who commands the wind and the waves, is with you and me. He's been there all along. And because he is in control, we don't have to be.

This is how worship sets us free from worry.

At its root, worry is faithlessness. It is saying, "I don't trust God to have my best interests in mind." Or, "I don't believe God is strong enough to take care of me."

Worry is a worship problem. It replaces the faith-filled worship of God with fear-driven worship of self. When you and I choose to worry, we are choosing to believe that *we* know better than God and if only he were as wise as we are, he would do things the way that we wanted. We foolishly set out to fix the situation with our own power and then freak out when our efforts turn up in vain. Finally, once we have exhausted ourselves from trying to keep the ship afloat, we run back to God and shout, "Save us! We are perishing!"

But what if we could bypass the freak-out? What if, instead of worrying, we chose to start with the awe and wonder of worship—"Who is this that even the wind and waves obey him!?"

Though the storm rages all around, you can choose to worship rather than worry because someone stronger than the storm is present with you and within you, taking care of you. He is able to change your situation, but even if he doesn't, you can rest knowing that he is completely sovereign, completely wise, and completely trustworthy.

The same faithlessness that fuels our fearful, "Don't you care that we are gonna drown?" compels us to ask, "Don't you care that we are gonna starve?"

Over the years, I have probably read Matthew 6:25–34 more than any other Scripture.

> Do not be anxious about your life, what you will eat or what you will drink, nor about your body, what you will put on. Is not life more than food, and the body more than clothing? Look at the birds of the air: they neither sow nor reap nor gather into barns, and yet your heavenly Father feeds them. Are you not of more value than they? And which of you by being anxious can add a single hour to his span of life? And why are you anxious about clothing? Consider the lilies of the field, how they grow: they neither toil nor spin, yet I tell you, even Solomon in all his glory was not arrayed like one of these. But if God so clothes the grass of the field, which today is alive and tomorrow is thrown into the oven, will he not much more clothe you, O you of little faith? Therefore do not be anxious, saying, "What shall we eat?" or "What shall we drink?" or "What shall we wear?" For the Gentiles seek after all these things, and your heavenly Father knows

that you need them all. But seek first the kingdom of God and his righteousness, and all these things will be added to you.

Therefore do not be anxious about tomorrow, for tomorrow will be anxious for itself. Sufficient for the day is its own trouble.

Worry looks at circumstances, but worship looks at truth. Worship combats worry by reminding us of the truth of God's character, his will, and his ways.

You don't know where your next meal is going to come from? Lost your job? Don't make enough money? Bills stacking up? Car broke down and you don't know how you're going to pay to fix it? You may feel powerless to control your situation, but look at how God feeds the birds and clothes the grass. Doesn't he care about you more than them? He is faithful. He cares. He will meet your needs.

Pride tempts us to gaze at our problems and feel the desperate anxiety of searching inwardly for the power to carry the heavy burden all by ourselves. However, worship is actively raising our gaze to the one who reigns above our problems and humbly reminding ourselves to be anxious about nothing, but in everything with prayer and thanksgiving, ask him for what we need (Phil. 4:6). We don't ignore the storm that is raging all around us, but instead, we cast all of our anxiety, worries, and cares upon Jesus because he cares for us (1 Pet. 5:7)!

When you and I choose to worship, we are reminding ourselves of the unchanging, unsurpassed, incomparable control of Christ. The very one who created money and financial systems—the one who gives us every talent, ability, and opportunity to begin with—is ultimately the one who provides for us. He holds the hearts of kings and rulers, presidents and governors in his hand and moves them as he desires like a stream of water to grow his people (Prov. 21:1).

There is no one who is stronger than our King Jesus, no one who can force his hand. He is completely sovereign and completely good. Storms will surely come, but because he has proven his character time and again, we can be sure that no storm will come into our lives outside of his sovereign hand allowing it for our good and for his glory. This is the amazing promise of Romans 8:31–32:

> If God is for us, who can be against us? He who did not spare his own Son but gave him up for us all, how will he not also with him graciously give us all things?

Jesus laying his life down to pay an infinite price for you is the ultimate statement that God keeps his promises. He is committed to you. He is stronger than the storm, and he is for you in the midst of it. And if God is for you, then there is never an appropriate time to worry. He is in control, so you don't have to be. Your faithlessness and pride can melt away in the presence of the Liberating King.

And there, as you worship in his presence, you are set free from worry.

Questions for Application and Discussion

1. What are you worried about right now? Think about those things and situations that consistently cause anxiety in you.

2. What lies do you believe about your situation, yourself, and God that are causing you to be anxious?

3. How would your life change if you were to replace the lies that were causing you to freak out with the truth of Scripture that would cause you to worship? Can you imagine a week where you choose not to worry but to worship instead? What is stopping you from trying that this week?

4

Learning to Be Brave

HOW THE LIBERATING KING
FREES US TO WALK BY FAITH
WHEN OUR WORLD IS UNRAVELING

And when they had sung a hymn, they went out to the Mount of Olives. Then Jesus said to them, "You will all fall away because of me this night. For it is written, 'I will strike the shepherd, and the sheep of the flock will be scattered.' But after I am raised up, I will go before you to Galilee." . . . Then he said to them, "My soul is very sorrowful, even to death; remain here, and watch with me." And going a little farther he fell on his face and prayed, saying, "My Father, if it be possible, let this cup pass from me; nevertheless, not as I will, but as you will."

Matthew 26:30–32, 38–39

And there appeared to him an angel from heaven, strengthening him. And being in an agony he prayed more earnestly; and his sweat became like great drops of blood falling down to the ground.

Luke 22:43–44

"YOU GUYS HAVE HAD A NAÏVE FAITH in the past and it has propelled you to do a lot of amazing, brave things. But now that you're no longer naïve, you have to learn to be brave knowing what you know now."

The words echoed in my heart as my wife and I sat across the room from Doug, our marriage counselor. For the first time in our lives, we had come to the end of ourselves and sat there disillusioned with the world. After taking a series of bludgeoning blows, we were decidedly crippled.

We had been going through the two hardest years of our lives, striving to connect with people who, in spite of our sincerest efforts, remained hostile to us. Not just indifferent, but overtly hateful. I had previously believed that if I remained humble and gentle with my words and actions, I could eventually live at peace with *anyone*. But in this case, it was truly not up to me. I was constantly walking around with the feeling that I was broken, asking what I could do differently to win over these people who so disdained me. I remember thinking, *How can these people be Christians?*

In the midst of this, I had unintentionally hurt the feelings of one of my best friends. For nearly a year, our friendship was certainly strained, if not nearly broken. I don't know if I have ever felt more misunderstood or hurt. I desperately longed to have the closeness of that friendship back but couldn't force the mending to happen any quicker. I felt helpless, disheartened. The weight of unforgiveness from my best friend was debilitating. I couldn't stop wondering how I could win that friend back.

On top of all of this, that same year my wife miscarried two children. The first on my birthday, the next at Christmas. I have no way of explaining the kind of devastation Amanda went through as we mourned the loss of two babies. There were days when I would come home from work and she would still be in bed, her pillow wet with tears.

I am an eternal optimist. People call me "Texas Happy." You will rarely see me without a smile on my face and a song on my lips. But for the first time in my life, I couldn't tell Amanda, "It's okay." I couldn't try to comfort her with some weak platitude or pithy statement. Because the truth was, it wasn't okay. I wasn't okay. I was utterly broken, my world unraveling.

"There is nothing okay about babies dying," Doug said. "Nothing okay about fellow Christians assaulting your character at every opportunity. Nothing okay about broken friendships. There are things that happen in this world *every single day* that are not okay. But don't use that to shut Jesus out. He wants to meet you in your brokenness and bring healing."

It's okay to not be okay.

Faith is not pretending everything is okay when it's really not. Faith is going to God when your world is unraveling. Faith is being brave knowing what you know now.

At Passover, just hours before he would hang on a cross, Jesus sat with his disciples, sharing a meal with them, loving them to the last, knowing what was in store. He told them how he would suffer, how he would be betrayed by Judas and abandoned by them all. He was not naïve about his body being broken and his blood being shed for them. He knew the cost, the pain he would endure. Yet he sang. He worshiped. He led his disciples in praise and then he walked with them to the garden, the very place where he knew Roman soldiers would come for him. This act of worship was as far from naïve faith as one can get. This was war.

Worship is not the naïve thing to do when faced with the choice of walking by faith or cowering in fear. It is not burying your head in the sand and pretending that everything is okay. Worship is staring at the gravity of the situation and throwing yourself upon the grace of the Savior. Worship is running to the Liberating King after all the disillusionment has set in and choosing to trust him, rather than being cynical. Worship makes us brave for the battle of unbelief and prepares us with courageous faith to follow wherever God leads.

The key word here is *wherever* God leads. Sometimes that doesn't make sense to us. Sometimes he calls you to give generously when your bank account says you can't. Sometimes he calls you to quit your white-collar, six-figure job and make a third of your normal salary so that you can help a church get organized, even though everything in your flesh says it's a bad idea. Sometimes he just says, as he did with Abraham, "Go . . . I'll tell you where when you get there."

In worship, the Spirit of Truth teaches us to trust that Jesus, the Truth himself, and his words of Truth are trustworthy. God will keep his word to shield and supply us as we walk with him. He reminds us of the old Sunday school proverb: "God equips those he calls. Where he guides, he provides."

John Wayne once said, "Courage is being scared to death, but saddling up anyway." This is the essence of faith.

Faith is not some cheap genie-in-a-bottle trick or get-rich-quick scam. It is not a manipulation mechanism to get God to bless you with a comfortable life. It doesn't purchase you health and wealth or protect you from suffering.

Faith says, "I'm scared to death, but I'm saddling up anyway. I want my life to count. I want God to use me. Not for what I get out of it, but for what *he* gets out of it."

Faith chooses to love even when you have been hurt; to forgive, even when the pain is still fresh.

Jim Elliot, an American missionary to the people of Ecuador, once penned in his journal, "He is no fool who gives what he cannot keep to gain what he cannot lose."

After moving to Ecuador in 1952, he married Elisabeth a year later and they began serving together in remote villages throughout the country. Convinced he needed to take the gospel to the Huaorani, a particularly savage group of people who had killed every "white man" who had ever made contact, Jim and four other missionary friends devised a strategy to build trust by showering the Huaorani with gifts dropped from a small plane and shouting, "We are your friends! We want to visit you!"

Once the time seemed right, they touched down and engaged the Huaorani face-to-face. A week later, on January 8, 1956, Jim and his four missionary friends were speared to death by the Huaorani.

In the wake of her husband's death, God healed Elisabeth's heart and enabled her to forgive. She began praying fervently for an opportunity to go live among the Huaorani people and share the love of Jesus. She knew the risks better than anyone. Hers were not naïve prayers. This was worship that stared in the face of loss and said, "This is not the end. God deserves to be glorified by these people too."

Finally, in 1958, God opened the door for Elisabeth and Rachel Saint, the wife of one of the other slain missionaries, to move into the Huaorani village. For two years, they unwaveringly loved and served the people who had killed their husbands. The entire village was changed as a result, and they placed their faith and trust in Jesus.

When you think you can't forgive, worship turns your gaze to the cross and says, "Yes, you can." When the mountain seems insurmountable, worship strengthens you to say, "With God . . ."

Even when you are in anguish over the task at hand, weary from carrying the burden deep inside your soul, worship reminds you that Jesus walked that same road as well. His hymns of praise at the Passover meal and groans of worship at Gethsemane gave him the strength to march to Calvary—not naïvely, but with the faith to see the joy set before him.

Most theologians believe that the Passover hymn Jesus led his disciples in would have been taken directly from Psalms 114–118. When Jesus needed the faith to walk in obedience, he sang God's Word. Can you hear him singing the words of Psalm 116:1–9?

> I love the LORD, because he has heard
>   my voice and my pleas for mercy.
> Because he inclined his ear to me,
>   therefore I will call on him as long as I live.
> The snares of death encompassed me;
>   the pangs of Sheol laid hold on me;
>   I suffered distress and anguish.

Then I called on the name of the LORD:
    "O LORD, I pray, deliver my soul!"

Gracious is the LORD, and righteous;
    our God is merciful.
The LORD preserves the simple;
    when I was brought low, he saved me.
Return, O my soul, to your rest;
    for the LORD has dealt bountifully with you.

For you have delivered my soul from death,
    my eyes from tears,
    my feet from stumbling;
I will walk before the LORD
    in the land of the living.

Faith is the fruit that comes from planting God's Word deep into your mind, mouth, and memory. In worship, the Spirit of Truth comes to you in a very unique way and nurtures the roots of God's faith-producing Word of Truth. He reorients your perspective from earthly logic to kingdom logic and gives you a bold confidence to do the unimaginable. He reminds you that nothing is impossible when the God who is able to do immeasurably more than you could ask or dream is with you.

Walking by faith is never a bad idea when your faith is fixed on a God whose power is unmatched. He is completely competent. His track record is perfect. He is steadfast in his will to accomplish his purposes through you.

Worship sets us free to have the kind of faith that everyone else thinks is crazy; it reminds us that when we follow Jesus, we can't lose. Our Liberating King has already won all the battles that matter. He is the Victor, the Champion, and when we walk with him, he leads us in *his* triumph.

When you worship in Spirit and Truth, you are set free to fail, because Jesus's victory defines you more than your failures. When you get hurt, he heals. When people reject you, he accepts you. When others are fickle, he is faithful. When circumstances are unsteady, he is unshakable. Though all other ground is sinking sand, you will always be able to sing, "On Christ the solid rock I stand!"

When you worship, pray, and meditate on who God is, what he has done, and who you are in light of that, you are emboldened in the light of this glorious truth: obeying God is never a mistake.

When God is with you, you can walk in obedience by faith no matter the call and no matter the consequences. In captivity or capsized boats, he is with you. In the lion's den and in the fiery furnace, he is with you. When you face giants or stand before godless kings, he is with you.

Sometimes God will call you to take the gospel to a hostile unreached people group, and sometimes the call will be to simply love your neighbor right next door. He may ask you to adopt children who desperately need a family, even if the finances aren't there, and you'll have to trust him to provide. Or he may simply say to be content with discipling the children within your home right now, for the glory of his name.

Sometimes God will call you away from the security of a job you love in order to move to a new city, but he won't tell you how you're going to get there until the time is right. Or he may call you to stay where you are, in a very difficult place, in order to use you and sanctify you there.

In worship, we are embracing the Lordship of Jesus. We are saying to him, "You are God—the highest and the first in my life—and you have the right to call me anywhere and ask anything of me. No matter what, my answer is yes."

At its core, worship is drawing near to the presence of God. It is the drive to be where Jesus is. It is the longing to go when he goes and stay when he stays. It is the cry of Peter, when he saw Jesus walking on the waves.

And in the fourth watch of the night [Jesus] came to them, walking on the sea. But when the disciples saw him walking on the sea, they were terrified, and said, "It is a ghost!" and they cried out in fear. But immediately Jesus spoke to them, saying, "Take heart; it is I. Do not be afraid."

And Peter answered him, "Lord, if it is you, command me to come to you on the water." He said, "Come." So Peter got out of the boat and walked on the water and came to Jesus. But when he saw the wind, he was afraid, and beginning to sink he cried out, "Lord, save me." Jesus immediately reached out his hand and took hold of him, saying to him, "O you of little faith, why did you doubt?" And when they got into the boat, the wind ceased. And those in the boat worshiped him, saying, "Truly you are the Son of God." (Matt. 14:25–33)

The worship-filled longing to be with Jesus produces faith in us to step out when he calls us to join him. When our faith falters, as it inevitably will, he takes our hand and lifts us up. Seeing and experiencing God's faithfulness gives us a rich history to look back on the next time he calls us to step out.

Imagine if Jesus took Peter back out in the boat that next week and called him to take a stroll on the water. Would the remembrance of his sinking feet be more powerful than the worship that overcame him when he realized, "Truly you are the Son of God"? Do you think he would have a hard time following Jesus's lead?

Worship sets us free to walk by faith by replacing our fears with the confidence of seeing God for who he is—sovereign, loving, wise, and fiercely devoted to us. His presence makes every excuse irrelevant. His power makes every obstacle just another opportunity.

David lived a life of faith, running after the heart of God in worship. Nonetheless, his life was turbulent and God called him to do many hard things. When his faith began to fail him, he would strengthen himself by remembering God's character, will, and ways. The Lord had always been faithful, so why would that change now?

> For who is God, but the LORD?
>   And who is a rock, except our God?—
> the God who equipped me with strength
>   and made my way blameless.
> He made my feet like the feet of a deer
>   and set me secure on the heights.
> He trains my hands for war,
>   so that my arms can bend a bow of bronze. . . .
>
> The LORD lives, and blessed be my rock,
>   and exalted be the God of my salvation.
>   (Ps. 18:31–34, 46)

This same God who walked with David walks with you now. Jesus was forsaken so that you would never be.

The world is broken, and many dark days are still ahead. There will be times when everything won't be okay. But in the midst of it all, you can find the freedom to walk by faith, worshiping in the presence of the ever-faithful God.

Questions for Application and Discussion

1. Where is God calling you to step out in faith right now?

2. What is stopping you from obeying? In what ways have the wounds of your past influenced your ability to walk by faith?

3. What lies do you believe about God that might be hindering you from trusting him? How can you replace those lies with the truth of Scripture and fuel your faith with worship in response to that truth?

5

Death to the Approval Vampire

HOW THE LIBERATING KING
FREES US TO LOVE OTHERS

But when the Pharisees heard that he had silenced the Sadducees, they gathered together. And one of them, a lawyer, asked him a question to test him. "Teacher, which is the great commandment in the Law?" And he said to him, "You shall love the Lord your God with all your heart and with all your soul and with all your mind. This is the great and first commandment. And a second is like it: You shall love your neighbor as yourself. On these two commandments depend all the Law and the Prophets."

Matthew 22:34–40

HAVE YOU EVER CONSIDERED how simple Christianity really is? People have always tried to muddy the waters and make things more complicated than they really are. But at its essence, this is what it means to follow Christ, true worship summed up in four small words: love God, love people.

Growing up, I often heard the Oprahesque platitude, "Before you can love anyone else, you have to learn to love yourself." To this day I hear believers reciting this like it is biblical truth, as though this message is at the heart of what Jesus was saying when he told us to love our neighbors as we love ourselves.

To be fair, there is some truth to this. Of course we cannot care for others if we are not caring for ourselves. But our problem isn't that we don't love ourselves enough; it's that we love ourselves too much, and it has made us insecure.

We are self-obsessed, myself included, constantly concerned about what other people are thinking about us, positioning ourselves for approval. Of course, this manifests itself differently for everyone.

Perhaps you feel the draw to puff yourself up with a facade of strength, putting your best foot forward and acting like you have it all together. You exaggerate the truth in order to make people think and speak well of you. You fight to be in the inner circle and then make a point to let others know that you are in it. You want to know everyone and be known by everyone, but the reality is that no one knows the real you. You have a million "friends," but no one to help you when you need it most.

Or perhaps you shrivel back in fear, scared to death that people will think poorly of you if you let the real you show. Your desire for approval paralyzes and secludes you from others in order to keep yourself protected. The ball is always in everyone else's court to pursue you for any kind of relationship, yet you wonder why no one invites you to spend time with them. Loneliness inevitably sets in.

Insecurity rarely leads to loving others well. If you and I are to follow Christ's command to love others, it's hard to do that well when we're using them to find our own value and worth—feeding off of them like some sort of approval vampire.

No one sets out to be an approval vampire. I have yet to meet a single person who would admit to that as his or her calling in life. Yet the longing for value—the thirst for approval—is universal. It's in all of us, an insatiable, eternal hunger that each of us are trying to quench.

Over the years, the longing for recognition has been a temptation I consistently have to fight and flee from. As awful as this sounds (and is), I see how God blesses someone else's ministry and instead of rejoicing for them, I immediately find myself wrestling with envious thoughts. Rather than praising God for what he is doing through them, I play the comparison game. I too want to be celebrated, respected, thought well of.

Someone once said, "Comparison is the thief of joy." It's hard to have true joy when you believe the lie that you deserve more or you don't feel like you're getting the approval your heart longs for.

As much as I would love to say that I have outgrown this struggle by now, I still have to remind myself of this one great truth every single day: I am approved of by God. This chapter is as much for me as it is for you.

Since the Garden of Eden, our wayward hearts have tried to take man's applause, affirmation, and acceptance and shovel them into the void of our hearts, hoping they will eventually fill it.

The problem is that an infinite God has created us with an infinite gap inside of our souls that *only* he can fill. Until we learn to find our worth deeply rooted in Christ, we will continually use the people we are called to love in order to find our own validation. And they will let us down. They will fail to give us the meaning our hearts long for, because this kind of burden is too great a weight for any human to carry.

If you think about it, looking to people who have the same void as you do and asking them to fill the void in you is like a blind person asking another blind person to lead him across the street in a real-life game of Frogger. It will crush you every time.

If you are going to live out the simplest form of Christianity, you need a confidence that doesn't come from loving yourself more or getting other people to love you, but from recognizing the inherent value that a loving God gave you when he made and remade you. If you want to fill the void in your soul and love people well, you need to look to someone who doesn't have the same problem you do.

Jesus had no void that needed filling. He was the definition of filled-to-overflowing. So when he came to this earth, he wasn't looking for people to help him find his meaning and worth. He didn't use them so that he could feel good about himself. He knew who he was—the Son of God, and God himself—and that deep, intimate knowledge enabled him not to be served, but to serve and love with no ulterior motives.

Though he had quite the busy itinerary and was constantly in front of people, healing, feeding, and teaching them, it wasn't the approval of the masses that drove him.

Immediately he made his disciples get into the boat and go before him to the other side, to Bethsaida, while he dismissed the crowd. And after he had taken leave of them, he went up on the mountain to pray. (Mark 6:45–46)

This passage from Mark follows right on the heels of a miracle. Jesus had just taken five loaves and two fish and fed five thousand men, along with their wives and children. That's kind of a big deal—the kind of thing that would break the internet these days. But he didn't wait for a standing ovation, or for people to tell him how great he was. He didn't need it. He was completely unmotivated by their applause because he had a greater affirmation in mind—to spend time in the presence of his Father who delighted in him.

Jesus didn't need anything from the crowd because worshiping in the presence of the Father reminded him of his truest identity and filled him with a joy that satisfied him more than all their praise could. He recognized that the desert of man's approval would only leave him thirsty, so he went to the only eternal, living fount of satisfaction.

Similarly, when Jesus's ancestor, King David, felt rejected and was fleeing from his enemies, he cried out, not with wailing woes, but in worship-filled hope. There in the wilderness, he sang the following:

> O God, you are my God; earnestly I seek you;
> my soul thirsts for you;
> my flesh faints for you,
> as in a dry and weary land where there is no
> water.
> So I have looked upon you in the sanctuary,
> beholding your power and glory.

Because your steadfast love is better than life,
   my lips will praise you.
So I will bless you as long as I live;
   in your name I will lift up my hands.

My soul will be satisfied as with fat and rich food,
   and my mouth will praise you with joyful lips,
when I remember you upon my bed,
   and meditate on you in the watches of the night.
      (Ps. 63:1–6)

Jesus was free to love others well because he didn't need anything from them. When he went to his Father in worship, he was reminded that he already had the only acceptance that really mattered.

David was free to love and lead his people because when he went to God in worship, he realized that, though for a time he was being rejected by men, he was still approved of by God. His value came not from how people viewed him or spoke of him, but from the one who had created him in his image.

Our Liberating King Jesus frees you and me to love others well because he himself knows both acceptance and rejection. Hebrews 4:15 says that "in every respect [he was] tempted as we are, yet without sin." He knows what it feels like to love the thrill of accolades and attaboys. He knows what it means to battle depression when people don't give you the attention you long for. Yet in the midst of the temptation to use people rather than love them, he fled to the throne of majesty in worship.

If you are ever going to have a hope of loving your neighbor as yourself and freedom from the poison of self-obsession, it has to begin with loving the Lord with all your heart, mind, and soul. When you draw near to the heart of God, he has a way of setting your world in the proper perspective—highlighting what really matters and what really doesn't.

Worship draws us away from ourselves and our own glory and fixes our gaze in its proper place—on the glory, beauty, and worth of our Creator. Worship reminds us that our greatest worth is found in the infinitely worthy one.

As you sing, pray, and meditate on the character of God, who he is and what he has done, you can't help but find yourself at the foot of the cross, the place where God put his ultimate stamp of worth on you. At the cross, Jesus purchased you with his own blood and definitively declared, "Mine!" over all who would place their trust in him.

Like Andy from *Toy Story* writing his name on Woody's boot to show ownership, value, and affection, Jesus has written his name on your heart to remind you who you are and *whose* you are. Furthermore, Isaiah 49:16 tells us that God has engraved us on the palms of his hands. We are his and he is ours.

This is astounding! How can it be that the God who made the universe and everything in it would care so much about the people who fail him every single day? How can it be that he would create mankind in his image knowing that we would choose a piece of fruit in the Garden of Eden over his all-satisfying presence? How can it be that God himself would come to dwell *with* us in the person of Jesus and then to dwell *in* us in the person of the Holy Spirit? This is simply *incredible!* It defies all logic.

Worship stands in awe of who God is, what he has done, and who we are in light of that, and it sings, "How marvelous! How wonderful is my Savior's love for me!" It proclaims with astonishment, "Amazing love! How can it be that you, my King, would die for me?"

Worship is our response to God, allowing us a glimpse of the unimaginable, a comprehension of the incomprehensible, a revelation of the infinite breadth and length, height and depth of the love of God.

This is the only love we will sing of for all eternity. The kind of undeserving, scandalous love that would cause the ever-holy God to come and lay down his life as a sacrifice to ransom for himself people from every nation, tribe, and tongue.

In spite of all your flaws and deficiencies, brokenness and hang-ups, you are chosen and dearly loved by God (Col. 3:12). Before you ever did anything good or bad, God chose to make you his own and predestined you for adoption (Eph. 1:4–5). You can't earn that and you can't lose it. The love of God toward his people is completely undeserved grace upon grace.

Worship sits in this truth, basking in its glory, savoring the taste of the unconditional approval that Christ earned for us! Worship sees the nail-scarred hands of the risen, reigning Christ welcoming us to himself with a warm embrace.

But here's the kicker—it doesn't terminate there. In 1 John 4:7–11, 18–19, John encourages us, saying:

> Let us love one another, for love is from God, and whoever loves has been born of God and knows God. Anyone who does not love does not know God, because God is love. In this the love of God was made manifest among us, that God sent his only Son into the world, so that we might live through him. In this is love, not that we have loved God but that he loved us and sent his Son to be the propitiation for

our sins. Beloved, if God so loved us, we also ought to love one another. . . .

There is no fear in love, but perfect love casts out fear. For fear has to do with punishment, and whoever fears has not been perfected in love. We love because he first loved us.

In Christ, we find a perfect love that gives us a new name and a new identity and compels us to love others, no matter how unloved we have felt in the past.

Some kids have fun nicknames growing up. For example, we call our son, Ethan, a variety of names like "Jack-Jack," "Dennis the Menace," and my personal favorite, "Hurricane Ethan." He is this incredibly energetic hurricane of a kid whom you can't help but love in the midst of all the chaos he stirs up because he just has this disarmingly cute little smile and bubbly personality.

I never had the luxury of a cool nickname. Growing up as the obese kid in school, classmates called me pretty cruel things like "Fatty" and "Tubby," just to name a few. My eighth grade gym class was particularly brutal. Kids would shout out, "Hang a donut in front of Tubby and he'll run faster!" On one occasion, our class was running on the track when some kids sprinted ahead and hid behind a bleacher with a pile of rocks. When I ran by, they began throwing rocks at me, shouting "Tubby! Tubby! Haha! Tubby's gonna cry!"

As I moved into high school I became the target of the varsity football team, who made it their goal to motivate me to lose weight. I got new, more crass nicknames. Walking down the hallways as a sophomore, some of the bigger senior classmen would walk by, shove me into a locker, and pour their soda all over me. "Why don't you get in the gym?"

Add that on top of the fact that my dad had just left our family, and I felt pretty worthless. I felt like I had no value whatsoever. I would lie on my bed at night staring at the ceiling, wondering if anyone would ever love me. And I determined that I would never feel this way again. I was not worthless, and I needed to prove it.

I began working out, eating right, and focusing on putting forth my best self. For years and years, I fought to make sure that no one ever doubted my value again. The problem was that I had become so driven by the approval of others that when I didn't have it, it drove me to depression. I may have been thinner, healthier, and more talented than before, but that void was still there. Other people couldn't fill it, and as long as I was looking for them to, I was just going to be miserable. I couldn't love others because I was constantly trying to use them to earn my approval.

Over time, God began to show me my wounds and bind them up. I couldn't pretend they weren't there. Even now, every time those feelings of worthlessness creep in, he confronts me with the lies I believe about myself and about him, reminding me that my worth isn't given to me by people but was definitively declared at the cross. That I am created in his image, purchased with his blood, adopted into his family, filled with his Spirit, and given an eternal inheritance in his kingdom. Day by day, I am growing in the understanding of who I am in Christ, and as I grow, I am able to truly love others well.

The more you feel the warm embrace of Christ and taste the approval that he purchased for you, the more you want that for others as well. The more you experience the security of being accepted in spite of all your faults, the more comfortable you are with who God made and remade you to be and the more confident and free you are in loving others.

When you love the Lord with all your heart, mind, and soul, that worship will naturally express itself outwardly in love toward those he created in his image. You begin to love those he loves. And not with some cheesy Hallmark love, but with the kind of sacrificial love that lays down your own preferences for the sake of another and treats others better than yourself. This kind of love isn't so concerned with getting worth from others as much as generously lavishing value on them.

Worship sets you free to love well because it removes the question of "Do I matter?" and moves you to ask, "How can I love like Christ? How can I give, serve, encourage, and build up my neighbor?" Worship drives out the fear of rejection and fills you with the confidence to risk loving people who might not love you back. It compels you to give to those who can't return the favor and constrains you from playing the joy-sucking comparison game.

Worship at its core is loving God and loving people, in that order. As God initiates worship in our hearts, we are drawn into his unconditional acceptance and enabled to love others with the confidence that can only come from time with him.

As you worship in the presence of the God who knows everything about you—the real you—all your insecurities melt away, and you are set free to love. So love well.

Questions for Application and Discussion

1. In what ways do you position yourself to gain approval from people? Are there any areas in your life that you

puff up or hide in order to be seen as more worthy of value and approval?

2. What are the past wounds in your life that have shaped an unhealthy or untrue view of yourself, God, and the world around you that you need to address? How are those wounds keeping you from loving others well?

3. How can you create rhythms of worship that consistently replace the lies you are tempted to believe with the truth of Scripture that God has fearfully and wonderfully made you and all those he is calling you to love?

6

Moving Beyond Warm Fuzzies

HOW THE LIBERATING KING
FREES US TO JOIN HIS MISSION

Now the eleven disciples went to Galilee, to the mountain to which Jesus had directed them. And when they saw him they worshiped him, but some doubted. And Jesus came and said to them, "All authority in heaven and on earth has been given to me. Go therefore and make disciples of all nations, baptizing them in the name of the Father and of the Son and of the Holy Spirit, teaching them to observe all that I have commanded you. And behold, I am with you always, to the end of the age."

Matthew 28:16–20

When they were released, they went to their friends and reported what the chief priests and the elders had said to them.

And when they heard it, they lifted their voices together to God and said, "Sovereign Lord, who made the heaven and the earth and the sea and everything in them. . . . Lord, look upon their threats and grant to your servants to continue to speak your word with all boldness, while you stretch out your hand to heal, and signs and wonders are performed through the name of your holy servant Jesus." And when they had prayed, the place in which they were gathered together was shaken, and they were all filled with the Holy Spirit and continued to speak the word of God with boldness.

Acts 4:23–24, 29–31

I BECAME THE MAN OF THE HOUSE way younger than I should have. When I was fifteen years old, my dad moved to Austin, Texas, and left me as the only guy in my home, watching over my mom and younger sister.

I really can't describe how I felt about it. Some days I was angry, some found me distraught, and other days I was completely hard and cold. But regardless of my particular mood and feelings, I was certainly in a crisis of belief.

My mom ended up moving us to Austin as well in order for my sister and me to maintain a relationship with our dad, and we moved into a duplex just a couple of blocks away from Bannockburn Baptist Church. (Having grown up in Baptist churches my whole life, I was excited to go to this church because *Braveheart* was my favorite movie, and the fields of Bannockburn are where the Scottish won their freedom.) It was there that I met Charlie Harrisberger.

Charlie, my youth pastor, stood a good foot taller than me and weighed about half what I did. I was five feet four, pushing three hundred pounds, and he was probably six feet four with something like 2 percent body fat. In many ways, he stepped in and became a dad to me. He would give me rides to church, pay for me to go to youth camp, and he was the one who gave me my first opportunity to lead worship.

Each Wednesday night, I came to the church hours early just to spend time with Charlie before our student service began. He was never annoyed or frustrated but patiently poured into me. Over time, he began to give me books to read. One of those books was *Let the Nations Be Glad* by John Piper. The book's core theme was incredibly appealing to me as a would-be worship leader. Here's a sample:

> Missions exists because worship doesn't. Worship is ultimate, not missions, because God is ultimate, not man. When this age is over, and the countless millions of the redeemed fall on their faces before the throne of God, missions will be no more.[1]

Worship is ultimate because God is ultimate. And because God is ultimate, as believers, we should want as many people as possible to be able to enjoy him forever! When God captures our hearts with a deep joy in his presence, we should want people to know that joy, that delight.

Ronnie Smith was the kind of guy who exhibited that joy.

My wife and I began attending The Austin Stone Community Church in Austin, Texas, in early 2004. We had gone through a rough first year of marriage but longed to draw near to God in the middle of our spiritual desert. We wanted something authentic, something real.

We decided to join a community group that was right down the road from us. One night, we showed up at the home of

Ronnie and Anita Smith just in time to begin a study through Romans. Ronnie's heart for worship immediately began to captivate me.

He was a chemist—brilliant in every respect—and had more Scripture memorized than anyone I have met to this day. More than anything, Ronnie wanted all the nations of the world to come to know and worship Jesus.

After a couple of years, we eventually moved away, but Ronnie and I stayed in touch on and off over the next few years. He never ceased to point me to the gospel and deepen my affection for Christ. One day out of the blue, I received a text message from Ronnie, saying something like, "On the other side of the world right now listening to your music. Encouraged by it as I worship along. As you can imagine, there's not a lot of Christian music over here."

It turned out that Ronnie and Anita had responded to God's call on their lives to take the gospel to the nations so that as many people as possible could know and worship Jesus. God moved them to Benghazi, where Ronnie taught chemistry, and together he and Anita loved the people of Libya. They knew that it would be dangerous, and that there would certainly be risk involved, but they wanted to be a blessing, to share the love of Christ with the people of Libya.

In December of 2013, Anita and their son had come home to the United States for the holidays, and Ronnie was scheduled to join them shortly after helping his students through their midterms. But on December 5, he was murdered— gunned down in the streets of Libya. Rather than retaliate, Anita responded with compassion, writing, "To his attackers, I love you and I forgive you. How could I not? For Jesus taught us to 'Love our enemies'—not to kill them or seek revenge. Jesus sacrificed His life out of love for the very people who killed him, as well as for us today. . . . Ronnie loved you because God loves you. Ronnie loved you because God loved him—not because Ronnie was great, but because God is so great."

It was worship of a great God that spurred Ronnie and Anita to love the people of Libya. God's glory compelled them to consider everything loss in comparison to knowing Jesus and making him known. God's unfailing love assured them of his presence with them, no matter what, and their confidence in his sovereignty set them free to live out his mission in the world, sacrificing much for the greater reward of hearing "Well done, good and faithful servants."

God's purpose in worship is not to make you feel warm fuzzies or give you some emotional high. It is to draw you near to him so that he might transform you and send you out to change the world with the good news of who he is and what he has done.

In worship, God communicates his unmatched beauty, power, and glory to you, and then he empowers you with a supernatural boldness and confidence to tell the nations that he saves and sets captives free! As you and I spread the gospel, he promises to be with us and in us all along the way, strengthening and encouraging us, even in the darkest of days. Though our earthly bodies may be killed and we may lose everything, our mission *cannot* fail, because God takes the ashes of even our death and loss to produce the life-giving fruit of salvation throughout the world.

Just before Jesus laid down his life for those whom he would set free, he told his followers,

Truly, truly, I say to you, unless a grain of wheat falls into the earth and dies, it remains alone; but if it dies, it bears much fruit. Whoever loves his life loses it, and whoever hates his life in this world will keep it for eternal life. If anyone serves me, he must follow me; and where I am, there will my servant be also. (John 12:24–26)

God takes fallen seeds and multiplies them into eternal life. He takes our sacrifice and loss and uses it to save the lost! Though you and I may never see the fruit this side of forever, we know that God's promise is true. His mission will not fail, and he is constantly inviting us to join him in it—to make his glory known to the peoples of the world, no matter the cost.

Worship draws near to God, sees him in all his holiness and brilliance, and longing for others to see him, cries out, "Here I am! Send me!" (Isa. 6:8). Worship sees infinite magnificence and can't help but share it with everyone. It looks at the threats, risks, and dangers of following Christ and dismisses them, saying, "Sovereign Lord, who made the heaven and the earth and the sea and everything in them . . . grant to your servants to continue to speak your word with all boldness" (Acts 4:24, 29).

When you pursue the heart of the Liberating King in worship, he shapes you to love what he loves—and he *loves* to liberate people from their bondage to sin, death, and hell. He moves you out of the self-worship of ease and comfort into the obedience of faith that sacrifices so that the nations can know him. He gives you a contagious joy in him and mobilizes you to spread that joy to all the peoples of the world, saying, "Let the nations be glad and sing for joy!" (Ps. 67:4).

Jesus loves the nations. He loves all people! No matter their language, skin color, or economic background, whether they live in the garbage cities of Guatemala or the leper colonies of India, Jesus wants them. The soccer mom across the street and the prostitute on the street corner, the Fortune 500 CEO and the restaurant employee who serves him lunch—Jesus knows them and loves them and is calling his people to tell them the Good News.

According to the Joshua Project, there are over sixty-five hundred unreached people groups in the world, consisting of over three billion people, who have never even *heard* the name of Jesus and have no access whatsoever to the gospel! These numbers are staggering! All the while, Jesus is beckoning us to go and tell them who he is and what he has done so that they may come to worship him and know the joy of his presence.

Think about it: the very last thing Jesus told his disciples—so important that he *made sure* to leave them with it right before he ascended to his throne in heaven—was to go out into the *whole* world and make disciples. That means across the street and across the globe. He wants people from everywhere!

Jesus has a mission and he *will* accomplish it! He doesn't need you, but he invites you to join him in this mission because he knows that the greatest joy you can experience will come from letting your worship work itself out on his mission. Your greatest delight will come from taking the message to as many people as possible so that one day men and women from everywhere will gather around the throne and join you in worshiping your Savior, crying out, "Worthy are you . . . for you were slain, and by your blood you ransomed people for God from every tribe and language and people and nation" (Rev. 5:9).

This is the scene of heaven. There will be no dividing walls of language or class or skin color. There will be no majority and minority races. None more privileged than another. No slave or free, poor or rich, sick or healthy, haves or have-nots. But every single knee will be bowed, singing praise to the Lamb who was slain to purchase them. Every person who places their trust in Christ will see the greatest beauty in all of existence, the Fountain of Majesty who flows with eternal life and glorious light, and we will worship with all the adoration that our heavenly bodies could possibly produce!

Worship here on earth is our foretaste of this. It is an appetizer to make us hungry for as many people as possible to taste and see that God is good. Worship ought to give us an urgent passion to not waste a single drop of the precious blood Jesus spilled because we were too lazy and self-focused or timid and terrified to tell people about his perfect sacrifice. Worship takes your attention off of yourself and puts it on those who need to hear. It beckons you to come die to self and then go make worshipers.

This is what Hebrews 12:2 speaks of, saying, "Jesus, the founder and perfecter of our faith, who for the joy that was set before him endured the cross, despising the shame, and is seated at the right hand of the throne of God." At the cross, Jesus was looking ahead to the moment when all those he purchased for himself will stand before his glorious throne in praise, and he will see what the price of his blood earned him—a purified bride full of people from every nation, tribe, and tongue. He suffered and was slain to receive the reward of all those who would trust in his work upon the cross and come delight in his presence for eternity.

Charles Spurgeon once famously said, "Every Christian is either a missionary or an imposter." That may sound strong, but his point is solid! As Christians, you and I are first and foremost worshipers. But in worship, as we encounter the Person of Truth in Jesus, are filled with the Spirit of Truth, and rehearse the Word of Truth, we are transformed into missionaries.

How could we not be? How could you see the risen, reigning Christ and not want to give your whole life to him? When you experience the scandalous grace of Jesus, how could you not want to tell everyone all that he has done for you? How can you hear that there are billions of people all over the world—from your neighbor next door to your neighbor in the remotest village of Africa—who have never heard the gospel, and be okay with that?

It's not okay! It's tragic! And God has invited you and me to be the ones to take this liberating gospel to them. He wants to use you, to send you. His message today is the same as it was at his ascension, "Go, make disciples of all nations." That commission hasn't changed in over two thousand years. And it won't change until he returns to call his family home.

Every time you come to God singing, praying, reading Scripture, or meditating on him in worship, Jesus is there, giving you his heart for the nations, spurring you on, helping you see the world through his eyes and love the world with his love. He wants to use you to tell everyone who he is and what he has done.

As you worship, may your response to him always, only, ever be, "Yes, Lord! Yes to anything you ask."

May the Liberating King captivate you with the truth of his love for the world and set you free to live on his mission.

May the Lamb who was slain receive the reward of his suffering.

Questions for Application and Discussion

1. In what way is God calling you to be a missionary in his plan to free the nations with the gospel?
2. What is stopping you from walking in obedience by faith? What lies do you believe about God and about yourself that would keep you from trusting him enough to walk with him in this way?
3. What would be the most effective way for you to build in time with God every day to replace those lies with the truth of Scripture and respond in worship that would free you to join with his mission?

7

The Noise of Our Songs

HOW THE LIBERATING KING
FREES US TO ACT JUSTLY

He has told you, O man, what is good; and what does the
LORD require of you but to do justice, and to love kindness,
and to walk humbly with your God?

Micah 6:8

Religion that is pure and undefiled before God, the Father,
is this: to visit orphans and widows in their affliction, and
to keep oneself unstained from the world.

James 1:27

AT SOME POINT IN TIME, singing became the primary action associated with worship. As a result, my most prominent role as a worship leader is to lead the gathered church in singing. After the services, I am typically approached by a number of people who encourage me, saying, "Good worship today."

I totally understand what they mean, but it does feel a bit narrowly focused. Singing is certainly worship, and probably one of its most powerful forms. When we sing, it seals truth into our minds and memories and connects the gospel to our affections in very unique ways. Singing takes words to new heights and depths that they can't go to on their own. Singing engages our heads and hearts like few things can, and when we gather to sing to God and one another, it should have a mobilizing effect on us.

Worship was never intended to terminate at your head and heart. It's a gift from God to engage your hands too, to set you free to act justly, love mercy, and walk humbly with him.

As crazy as it may sound, I had been leading worship for six years or so before I read the book of Amos for the first time. My community group had just finished up a study in Romans and wanted to go through an Old Testament book. We decided on Amos and dove in the next week.

Chapter 5 ended up being a crossroads that changed my life forever. As a worship leader, it's difficult for me to hear God tell his people, "Get away from me with the noise of your songs, I don't even want to hear them anymore" (Amos 5:23, author's paraphrase). Those are some strong words that tend to make you perk up and examine your life and ministry.

My wife and I began to wrestle with how we might rearrange our lives to "let justice roll down" like a stream of refreshment to the least of these whom Jesus loves so dearly (Amos 5:24).

This wasn't an easy task. We were making next to nothing at the time. We had gotten married very young, and we had a little baby girl and another one on the way. So the idea of being generous with our income was a hard one to swallow. But as we studied God's Word and prayed together, it became increasingly obvious that God was leading us to step out in faith and follow his example of generosity.

I knew that there was a deep connection between what I sang and how I lived, so I needed to be singing about this. But because there seemed to be a lack of worship songs that talked about God's love for justice, mercy, and compassion, I began to write more and more in that vein. It's amazing how God used those songs to change my heart, life, and ministry over the years that followed. Little by little, our lives began to reflect God's heart for the broken.

We began to partner with Compassion International, not only by sponsoring three children through their program, but also by giving other people an opportunity to respond in worship to God's generosity toward them by helping rescue children out of poverty in Jesus's name. To this day, everywhere I travel to lead worship, I encourage people to not just sing songs but to worship through acting justly.

As we did this more and more, God began to turn our hearts toward adoption. We would pray and search the Scriptures, and God used that to increasingly illuminate the wonder of our own adoption in Christ. The more we worshiped in response to that glorious truth, the more we longed to live like Jesus lived and let our lives truly reflect his glory to the world. We wanted to be a tangible picture of the gospel of what God did for us in Jesus Christ.

So in 2011, after mountains of paperwork, months of fund-raising, and millions of prayers, we brought two incredible sons home from Ethiopia. Our lives have never been the same.

The more you draw near to God, beholding him in worship, the more you become like him. You begin to love what he loves and hate what he hates. He loves the least of these and hates fatherlessness. He loves the broken and hates brokenness. He loves the poor and needy, binds up the brokenhearted, heals the sick, and sets the captive free. The Liberating King came to put an end to our slavery to sin, death, and the devil. For freedom he set us free.

Seated on his throne in heaven, Jesus saw our need and had compassion. He got up from his throne, left all the glory of eternal, unbroken communion with the Father and the Holy Spirit, wrapped himself in flesh, and dwelt among us. The light of the world broke through the darkness to come and rescue us.

In Matthew 9, as Jesus went throughout all the cities and villages, he looked out and saw people harassed and helpless, like sheep without a shepherd, and he was filled with compassion. He had mercy on them, healing and caring for them. The same Holy Spirit that filled him fills us now as we look to him in worship. He shows us Jesus and helps us to live as he did.

Though Jesus was rich, yet for our sake he became poor so that through his poverty we might enjoy his incomparable riches for all of eternity.

His love equaled sacrifice. His mercy cost him everything, even his own life. The one who created us bought us back from our bondage with the price of his own blood. Though we were fatherless, he made us sons and daughters so that he might be our greatest treasure.

Worship is treasuring Jesus above all things. He knows that your greatest good is found in him alone, so he isn't shy about telling you to put your treasure where your heart *should be*, to actively take the wrecking ball of truth to all the things that would compete in your heart for the highest place of affection.

Your heart and mine desperately cling to our riches, and we *must* constantly remind ourselves how quickly they can fail us. We so militantly hoard our time because of how precious it is, but we must remember that our time can instantly be cut short by a single unexpected turn of events. We can lose everything in the blink of an eye. Nothing in this world is guaranteed; no investment is secure. There is only one in whom you can trust and not be let down.

God tells you to store up your treasure in heaven because he knows that when you invest in his kingdom, you will always gain an eternal reward. There is no way you can be robbed of that promise because it's guaranteed by the one who owns all the wealth in the world, who invented time and gave you your talents. He wants you to fight for your heart's ultimate joy by putting your treasure where his heart is—with the least of these.

Worship is about beholding the God who rescues the poor and needy; praising him for his sacrifice, mercy, generosity, and eternal power that saved you when you were helpless to save yourself; and then letting your praise overflow into action. The more you draw near to him, the more you begin to reflect his glory to the world by putting his character on display in your own life.

As you are increasingly astonished at his mercy, he will compel you to act mercifully. As you grow more and more amazed at his compassion, he will fill your heart with compassion for others. As you stand in awe over his perfect love and justice, he will set you free to act justly and move your heart toward love for the least of these.

Worship is more than words, more than songs. But our words and songs in worship move us to give to those who can't give back and love those who are loveless. The act of worship is an act of asking God to move the hearts of his people to meet the needs of the poor. It's pleading that our lives would be an echo of his heart to care for the broken and the hurting of this world and then acting on that prayer.

In worship, you're asking the Liberating King to use you as an instrument of his mercy, justice, and compassion and make you a vessel that distributes his unending freedom to the world.

Perhaps God is calling you not to invest that tax return into a pool for your backyard, but to help build a well for a village in Africa that doesn't have clean water, and in doing so, share the gospel of what Christ has done for you. Perhaps God is telling you to use your Christmas bonus, not to give your kids tons of toys they will be bored of within a month, but to buy coats, socks, and shoes for the homeless in your city and partner with an organization to distribute them. Or what if he is asking you to simply save a little bit each month to support a missionary, sponsor a child through Compassion, give to help a family adopt an orphaned child, or even adopt a child yourself?

I am not saying that we as believers don't get to enjoy the resources that God gives us. I am saying that he has set us free to set others free. He has shown you kindness that you might show kindness, and he has blessed you that you might be a blessing. He has lavished you with glorious, undeserved grace upon glorious, undeserved grace so that you might reflect his glorious grace to a world that has no categories for it. When people see the church actually being the church—actually following Jesus and living the way Jesus lived, bringing refreshment to a desperate world—they will see the glory of God on display.

Ultimately we can sing all we want, but if our worship is not more than songs, it is pointless. Look at the passion with which Jesus talks about this:

> When the Son of Man comes in his glory, and all the angels with him, then he will sit on his glorious throne. Before him will be gathered all the nations, and he will separate people one from another as a shepherd separates the sheep from the goats. And he will place the sheep on his right, but the goats on the left. Then the King will say to those on his right, "Come, you who are blessed by my Father, inherit the kingdom prepared for you from the foundation of the world. For I was hungry and you gave me food, I was thirsty and you gave me drink, I was a stranger and you welcomed me, I was naked and you clothed me, I was sick and you visited me, I was in prison and you came to me." Then the righteous will answer him, saying, "Lord, when did we see you hungry and feed you, or thirsty and give you drink? And when did we see you a stranger and welcome you, or naked and clothe you? And when did we see you sick or in prison and visit you?" And the King will answer them, "Truly, I say to you, as you

did it to one of the least of these my brothers, you did it to me." (Matt. 25:31–40)

He goes on to say that if you didn't care for the least of these, you weren't a believer to begin with and he will say he doesn't know you. These are strong words!

He is not saying that if you want to earn your salvation, you will care for the poor—as if earning salvation is even possible! No, he is saying that if he has truly set you free from your own slavery, if you have truly tasted the freedom his sacrifice earned for you, your response will be to worship him, not just by thinking good thoughts and singing good songs about him, but by living a life of mercy, justice, and compassion. If you have experienced his love, you will love as he loves. You will be passionate about what he is passionate about.

Every moment of every day, the world is trying to convince you to look out for number one. These lies keep you in the bondage of your own idols of comfort and control. Worship is actively fighting against the lies and replacing them with the truth. But you must refuse to be content with simply singing songs about a completely just and merciful God and begin to let the truth of those songs infiltrate your life.

Let the Spirit of Truth fill you in worship and supernaturally cause your affections to move you to action. Let the Word of Truth fill your mind, mouth, and memory, giving you eyes to see, ears to hear, and feet to move.

Look to the Liberating King, the Truth himself, and see the depth of love he has shown you. You were the lost, lonely, and loveless. You were the helpless, hungry, and homeless. You were the orphan, the alien. But he came and gave himself for you. He laid down his life that you might have it. He gave everything that all the riches of heaven would be yours.

Sing about that! Think about it all the time! Dwell on the riches that you have in Christ and abandon yourself to him in complete adoration and thanksgiving for all that he has done for you! Worship him with all you are and let that worship express itself outwardly, walking in the obedience of awe-filled faith and trust. Let your life reflect the glorious grace of God, ever proclaiming, "More than words! More than songs!"

This is the kind of pure and holy religion that the Liberating King delights in.

This is worship.

Questions for Application and Discussion

1. In what ways would your life change if you began to see acts of justice and mercy as worship?

2. What are some ways that you can be involved in caring for the least of these right now? What opportunities are before you? What are you passionate about?

3. God has blessed you to make you a blessing to others. What are the resources that you have to begin being a blessing to the world around you? What are the low-hanging fruits, the natural opportunities? Or is God potentially calling you to move beyond what is convenient to be a blessing outside your comfort zone?

8

The Majesty We Long to Behold

HOW THE LIBERATING KING
FREES US FROM THE MISCONCEPTION
THAT THE WORLD REVOLVES AROUND US

In the year that King Uzziah died I saw the Lord sitting upon a throne, high and lifted up; and the train of his robe filled the temple. Above him stood the seraphim. . . . One called to another and said: "Holy, holy, holy is the LORD of hosts; the whole earth is full of his glory!"

And the foundations of the thresholds shook at the voice of him who called, and the house was filled with smoke. And I said: "Woe is me! For I am lost; for I am a man of unclean lips, and I dwell in the midst of a people of unclean lips; for my eyes have seen the King, the LORD of hosts!" Then one of the seraphim flew to me, having in his hand a burning coal that he had taken with tongs from the altar. And he touched my mouth and said: "Behold, this has touched your lips; your guilt is taken away, and your sin atoned for."

And I heard the voice of the Lord saying, "Whom shall I send, and who will go for us?" Then I said, "Here I am! Send me."

Isaiah 6:1–8

I AM BORDERLINE ADDICTED TO TRAVEL. I can't get enough of it. I love the feeling of waking up in a new place and discovering all that it has to offer. Standing in the center of ancient cities and staring at the remnants of centuries-old architecture. Walking the luminous streets of Times Square at midnight. Feeling the sand under my toes as I look out at miles upon miles of ocean kissing miles upon miles of sky. Having a picnic under the Eiffel Tower. Breathing the crisp air at the top of a snowcapped mountain, looking down at the vast expanse of earth that surrounds me on every side. Taking the ferry across the Bosphorus in Istanbul. Sipping the greatest coffee in the world in Addis Ababa.

These things have a way of making us feel incredibly small, yet not belittling us. They humble us not by humiliating us but by helping us see the grandness that we get to be part of. A grandness that includes us but isn't about us. We are one small piece of something much, much bigger.

There are *three hundred billion* observable stars in the Milky Way galaxy. Three hundred billion. That number alone is impossible for me to comprehend! But that's just the makeup of one galaxy in a universe that is thought to have over one hundred billion galaxies! And in those one hundred billion galaxies, it is estimated that there are probably around seventy *billion trillion* stars. That's seven plus twenty-one zeros! It's unfathomably awe-inspiring. The universe is bigger than even my wildest dreams can imagine—millions upon millions of miles wide—and humankind occupies one minute, infinitesimal corner of it.

We don't stay up at night, gazing into the heavens so that we can stand in awe of ourselves. There is an innate longing inside your soul and mine to gaze upon majesty, to behold glory and suspend the false belief, if but for a moment, that we are the center of the universe.

Though every marketing company and romantic comedy tells us that the world revolves around us, we know deep down that if that's true, we are all in trouble. There is only one who created all things out of nothing but his imagination. Only one on whom everything hinges and hangs. He spoke creation into being by his word of power, for his glory. Colossians 1:16–17 tells us the following:

> By him all things were created, in heaven and on earth, visible and invisible, whether thrones or dominions or rulers or authorities—all things were created through him and for him. And he is before all things, and in him all things hold together.

Jesus is the definition of greatness, the majesty our hearts long to behold, the one true standard of glory by which we measure all other glories. And in the light of his glory, all the lies of false glory are exposed.

When I was a kid, there wasn't a single football team that could compare with the Dallas Cowboys. They were on top of the world. I would watch their games with my dad and collect as much Cowboys paraphernalia as I could get my hands on. From posters to T-shirts to little toy helmets, if there was a silver star on it, I wanted it.

One particular year, my town's high school basketball team took the state championship by storm. They were crazy good for a bunch of teenage ballers when compared to a bunch of other teenage ballers.

Later that year, our school brought in the Dallas Cowboys to play our basketball team in a benefit tournament to help raise money for cancer research. I couldn't tell you how much money they raised, but I am pretty sure the Cowboys beat us by like a hundred points. Our players looked like a bunch of little kindergartners compared to them. It didn't matter that football was their main sport, they *slaughtered* us without breaking a sweat.

My dad was the high school math director, so he had access to the locker room and took me back to meet the players. All of a sudden, I became completely unaware of myself as I looked up at those giants and stood in awe. My perspective about greatness had completely changed.

This is what worship does for you. It changes your perspective of greatness. It draws your gaze away from yourself and fixates upon something infinitely more glorious. It humbles you.

Ever heard the saying, "Humility isn't thinking less of yourself. It's thinking of yourself less"? Worship has that effect on you. It disarms you of the self-seeking, self-serving pride that your flesh thrives on. When you stand before the infinitely majestic God, it reminds you what, or more specifically *who*, everything in existence is really all about. It's not about the person on your driver's license. It is about the one in whom you live and move and have your being (Acts 17:28).

Worship is the cry of John the Baptist: "He must increase, but I must decrease" (John 3:30). When you worship, you're joining with this cry and rebelling against the pride that would love to see it the other way around. You're actively deposing yourself from the throne of your heart, lifting Jesus to his rightful place there, and falling to your rightful place at his feet.

As you worship, God is with you in a very real way. This is not a hypothetical situation—God is with you! The very God who created planets and stars, and holds them all in his hands. The one who made electrons and protons, atoms and elements, gravity and inertia. This is the God you're encountering when you come to him in worship—praying, singing, and meditating on who he is and what he has done. Pride simply cannot exist in his presence. His glory is too massive to be minimized with self-centeredness. His holiness crushes all self-righteousness.

Look at Isaiah. In terms of godliness, he was a pretty big deal. He was a prophet, the mouthpiece of the living God. Considering he lived among a people who were running from God, it would have been easy for him to compare himself to their standard, to get caught up with himself and start believing his own press.

By human standards, Isaiah was about as righteous as you could get, but in Isaiah 6, when he stands in the presence of the three-times-holy God, he can't help but recognize how much those standards fall short. The angels are singing at the top of their lungs about how incredibly glorious God is, and Isaiah is undone, wrecked at the sight of it all. As he sees the image of perfection, he can't help but fall to his face and weep because the chasm between God and himself is far too great for him to bear.

God wanted to use Isaiah to change the world, but Isaiah had to realize he would have no bragging rights here—no room for boasting. So in his kindness, God comes to Isaiah, revealing his glory in a way that humbles Isaiah to his rightful place, and then God immediately extends his hand of atoning grace. The King over all creation graciously destroys the pride in Isaiah's heart by showing himself as the only worthy one, and then lifts Isaiah's head by freely bestowing unearned worth upon him. Once the work of humbling Isaiah is done, God calls him to join in his mission.

The same is true for us. God opposes the proud but gives grace to the humble (James 4:6). If you would be part of the glorious mission he has for you, you must humble yourself. Worship is one of the greatest gifts that God has given to you so that you might think rightly—not too highly or too lowly of yourself—in light of his matchless glory.

As you rehearse the truth of his word in your songs and prayers and meditation, you are reminding yourself of how completely perfect he is and of the righteousness that you have because you are hidden in him. As you worship, the Spirit fills you with a glory that is not your own and reminds you of your greatest identity: you are an adopted son or daughter of God, not because you earned it, but because Christ earned it for you at the cross.

Your value is not in anything that you bring to the table, but in the person and work of Jesus. He formed you, called you, saved you, and adopted you by his power and for his glory. He did it all from the beginning to the end. Ephesians 2:1, 4–9 says:

You were dead in the trespasses and sins. . . . But God, being rich in mercy, because of the great love with which he loved us, even when we were dead in our trespasses, made us alive together with Christ—by grace you have been saved—and raised us up with him and seated us with him in the heavenly places in Christ Jesus, so that in the coming ages he might show the immeasurable riches of his grace in kindness toward us in Christ Jesus. For by grace you have been saved, through faith. And this is not your own doing; it is the gift of God, not as a result of works, so that no one may boast.

It is quite humbling to realize that your approval before God is not due to anything you have done or could ever do. You were dead and hopeless. Dead people have no power to even call for help, let alone roll the stone away from their own grave. But because God is who he is, he sent the same Spirit that rolled Jesus's stone away to waken us to life that we might praise his glorious grace.

Worship is the only fitting response when you see what Jesus did to bring you from death to life. When you see who you were and who you are apart from the grace of God, it simultaneously produces humility and dignity in you. It sets you free to be humble by telling you how messed up you are and yet how loved you are at the same time. It reminds you that God has graciously allowed you to be part of something bigger than you that isn't about you. It allows you to stand on the endless horizon of God's glory and lift your hands in praise toward the sky of his infinite wonder because you get to be a speck on the everlasting spectrum of his majesty.

It's been all about Jesus all along.

You were an enemy—*he* made you a friend.

You were dead in your sins—*he* gave you a life that you can't lose.

You were an alien with no home—*he* gave you a home that can't be taken away.

You were helplessly broken—*he* filled you with hope and made you whole.

You were poor—*he* made you rich with a glorious heavenly inheritance.

You were blind—*he* gave you eyes to see the beauty of his majesty forever.

You were a wretch—*he* gave his life to make you his treasure.

Your body was formed from the dust and will wither and decay—*he* will give you a perfect, glorified heavenly body that will never know sickness or pain or arthritis or cancer or fatigue.

Your talents, riches, looks, and . . . well, everything else were given to you by *him*, and *he* can take them away at any time.

This life is not about you, and when you truly grasp that, you will be free to live for the things that will matter for eternity.

Come humble yourself in worship before the Eternal One and remember that though you are a mere breath, your breath matters. Stand amazed that though you are a vapor, your vapor can count for something infinite. Come join in with the song of eternity past and eternity future—"Not to us, oh Lord, but to Your name be the glory!"

Questions for Application and Discussion

1. In what areas of your life do you struggle with pride? Where are you tempted to make the world revolve around you?

2. How can you build rhythms of worship into your life that intentionally remove yourself from the throne of your heart and put God in his rightful place there?

3. In what ways would actively replacing the lies you believe with an increasingly massive view of God's glory change the way you live? What would your life look like if it truly revolved around God's perfection, priorities, and purposes? How can you begin to move in that direction?

9

Ten Looks at Jesus

HOW THE LIBERATING KING
FREES US FROM THE CYCLE OF SIN

[God's] invisible attributes, namely, his eternal power and divine nature, have been clearly perceived, ever since the creation of the world, in the things that have been made. So they are without excuse. For although they knew God, they did not honor him as God or give thanks to him, but they became futile in their thinking, and their foolish hearts were darkened. Claiming to be wise, they became fools, and exchanged the glory of the immortal God for images resembling mortal man and birds and animals and creeping things. . . . They exchanged the truth about God for a lie and worshiped and served the creature rather than the Creator, who is blessed forever! Amen.

Romans 1:20–23, 25

Again, the devil took him to a very high mountain and showed him all the kingdoms of the world and their glory. And he said to him, "All these I will give you, if you will fall down and worship me." Then Jesus said to him, "Be gone, Satan! For it is written, 'You shall worship the Lord your God and him only shall you serve.'" Then the devil left him, and behold, angels came and were ministering to him.

Matthew 4:8–11

I THINK I WEPT THE FIRST TIME I watched Disney's *Aladdin*, when I heard Aladdin tell the Genie, "You're free." To see the Genie's reaction as the shackles fell off his wrists and he gazed at the lamp in his hands that once held him captive—it was like nothing could stop him anymore. For the first time in his existence, he was experiencing life outside of bondage.

With all the Genie's power, no matter how he tried, he was still powerless to free himself. He needed the master to come to him and declare over his life, "You're free."

Though I'm writing about a children's movie, there are remarkable similarities to be found between it and the situation we find ourselves in. If you're rusty on your Disney movies, the climax of *Aladdin* shows the villain, Jafar, succumbing to the tempting allure of power—the longing to be God—and in doing so choosing the chains of captivity, just like our parents, Adam and Eve. As their descendants, we were born into that same slavery, held prisoner by sin and death, and each of us has chosen to exchange the glory of the ever-blessed Creator for something he created—namely ourselves.

At its core, sin is a worship issue. It is falling short of the glory of God, replacing the ever-glorious one with something far less-than. It is believing the lies that constantly surround us, placing ourselves at the center of our own affections and worshiping the wrong things. In doing so, we willingly place the shackles of sin upon ourselves.

Robin Williams was my favorite actor. He was brilliantly witty, and no one could make me laugh the way he did. In 2014, the world collectively mourned as reports of his suicide swept the news. To help cope with the pain, the internet erupted with memes showing the chains falling off the Genie. The captions read "You're free," as though Robin Williams had finally found the freedom he was depicting all those years earlier. He was a slave to his own brokenness, bound by the hopelessness of sin. And that inescapable bondage eventually robbed him and all the world of the beauty of his life.

No matter how sophisticated, stout, or sly we may be, we cannot break these impossible chains. We can't escape with lighthearted humor and endless jokes. We can't pretend our way out of it. We need a miracle. We need a Savior who is stronger than we are to set us free, not someone bound like us. As we come to God in worship, this is what he does for us. Our Liberating King sets us free from the bondage of sin—free to be holy.

In worship you are singing, praying, and meditating on the Word of God, and actively seeking to let the Word of God dwell in you richly as you submit to its authority over your life. You are purposefully inviting the Spirit of Truth to come and fill you, illuminating and applying God's Word to your heart so that you can respond in faith-filled obedience.

The Holy Spirit, whom Jesus sent to us, convicts the world of sin and helps God's people pursue holiness. He convinces us of the truth, enables us to repent, and shows us Jesus—the way, the truth, and the life. All the while, he is taking out our heart of stone and giving us a heart of flesh, replacing our old affections with new ones, and removing our desires for things that would only steal from us in order to fill us with longing for the ever-blessing, ever-blessed Giver.

As you worship, you are asking the Holy Spirit to inhabit your praises, fill you up, and empower you to "not present your members to sin as instruments for unrighteousness, but present yourselves to God as those who have been brought from death to life, and your members to God as instruments for righteousness" (Rom. 6:13).

The Spirit encounters you in worship and reminds you of this counterintuitive, but eternally logical truth.

Your hands weren't made for sin, but rather to raise in worship.

Your eyes weren't made for lust, but rather to gaze upon the beauty and majesty of God.

Your mind wasn't made to obsess over stuff that's just gonna kill you in the end.

Instead, you were created to use your body to worship Jesus, the only one who gives eternal life.

As you meditate on God's character, will, and ways, you are replacing earthly logic with heavenly logic and exchanging old affections for new and better ones.

When Jesus was in the wilderness, Satan came to him and tempted him by appealing to his earthly logic. If Jesus would just worship him, Satan would essentially deliver him from having to go to the cross. Jesus wouldn't have to die to save his people, Satan would simply give them to him, if only Jesus would worship him. What a deal, right?

I can just see the smooth salesman trying to pitch this idea to the Son of God. But Jesus knew that no one deserved worship except his Father. So rather than clinging to earthly logic to argue his way out, he recognized the spiritual battle and fought with a spiritual weapon. By the power of the Spirit of Truth that lived in him, he took up the Word of Truth and allowed it to saturate his mind, mouth, and memory. He withstood the temptation, and the enemy fled from him.

This is how worship sets us free to be holy. As we worship, we are submitting ourselves to God and declaring war on Satan. We are resisting him that he might flee from us (James 4:7). We are saying, "God alone is worthy of worship. I will not exchange his glory for another."

Your enemy doesn't have a lick of truth in him. He is a murderer, thief, and liar and has been since the beginning (John 8:44). He has been at this game for thousands of years and is an expert at it. He knows just how to tempt you and appeal to the sinful flesh within you. Then, as soon as you fail, he is there to condemn and accuse you.

This cycle never ends: tempt, accuse, tempt, accuse, tempt, accuse.

If he can get you to believe that your greatest identity is your sin, defining you by your failures and causing you to measure yourself by your own lack of merit, then he can break your will to strive for holiness.

The accuser wants you thinking you're just another sinner. You were born this way and you can't help it. He doesn't want your eyes on Christ. He wants your eyes on your sin. He wants you feeling hopelessly helpless, drowning in a sea of guilt and shame rather than running to the gracious Savior. But in worship, the Lifter of your head comes to you and raises your eyes to see the Suffering Servant upon the cross, paying for your sin—the risen Christ, conquering death for your sake.

The Scottish pastor Robert Murray M'Cheyne said, "For every look at yourself, take ten looks at Christ."[1] This is what it means to fight your sin with worship. Rather than carrying the weight of your sin, trying to take care of it yourself and slowly but surely sinking into the depths of despair, run to Christ and bring your burden to him. He will give you rest. His yoke is easy and his burden is light (Matt. 11:28–30).

David was a man after God's heart, and yet with all his passion to follow God by faith, he messed up in some pretty outrageous ways. This guy cheated with his friend's wife and then killed him when they found out she was pregnant with David's kid. That's like really bad soap opera kind of stuff.

But when God confronted David with his sin, rather than wallowing in despair, David remembered the mercy of God and sang a song of confession. He knew he had messed up, but even his deepest, darkest sin could be washed white as snow. So, he sang the song of Psalm 51:

> Have mercy on me, O God,
>   according to your steadfast love;
> according to your abundant mercy
>   blot out my transgressions.
> Wash me thoroughly from my iniquity,
>   and cleanse me from my sin!
>
> For I know my transgressions,
>   and my sin is ever before me.

Against you, you only, have I sinned
   and done what is evil in your sight,
so that you may be justified in your words
   and blameless in your judgment. . . .

Purge me with hyssop, and I shall be clean;
   wash me, and I shall be whiter than snow.
Let me hear joy and gladness;
   let the bones that you have broken rejoice.
Hide your face from my sins,
   and blot out all my iniquities.
Create in me a clean heart, O God,
   and renew a right spirit within me.
Cast me not away from your presence,
   and take not your Holy Spirit from me.
Restore to me the joy of your salvation,
   and uphold me with a willing spirit. . . .

O Lord, open my lips,
   and my mouth will declare your praise.
For you will not delight in sacrifice, or I would give it;
   you will not be pleased with a burnt offering.
The sacrifices of God are a broken spirit;
   a broken and contrite heart, O God, you will not
      despise. (vv. 1–4, 7–12, 15–17)

This is your opportunity when you sin. To come, repent, and be set free by the grace and compassion of a God who is slow to anger and abounding in steadfast love (Num. 14:18).

He doesn't do this by ignoring your sin. That would be unjust. No, he justly forgives every sin by nailing it to the cross of Christ. Jesus bled and died so that you would no longer remain in your sin, but be set free from it. He paid the debt of death that your sin had earned by taking the cup of God's wrath and drinking it down to the last drop.

Even when you were helpless to change, Christ gave everything to rescue you. When you worship in the presence of his glory, in light of his truth, the Spirit transforms you from one degree of glory to the next—even into Christ's own glorious image (2 Cor. 3:18).

When you are tempted to sin, you can run to Christ in worship and hide yourself in the refuge of his strength. When you are tempted to speak harshly or gossip behind someone's back, you can come to him and praise him that it was not his harsh words but his kindness that led you to repentance (Rom. 2:4). When you are tempted to lust, you can meditate on the beauty and majesty of God and remember his promise that the pure in heart would be blessed to see him (Matt. 5:8)! When you're fighting anxiety about your finances and are struggling to not be consumed with worry, you can worship by remembering that God will always provide for his own (Matt. 6:25–33).

And when you fail—because sometimes you will—you can run to Christ and confess, knowing he will cleanse you from all unrighteousness (1 John 1:9).

His call to you is not to do better and try harder. It's not to pull yourself up by your bootstraps and fix yourself. No, the Savior beckons you to come and worship, to rest in his finished work upon the cross. When he said, "It is finished," he wasn't lying. There is nothing left to be done because he did it all.

The truth is that any righteousness you could earn for yourself isn't really righteousness at all. All your "holiness" counts for nothing when you stand before an infinitely holy

God, unless your righteousness is hidden in him. If you aren't made completely perfect by the perfect work of the perfect Christ at the cross, then all your striving is filthy rags—it's rubbish. You're like the Genie, desperate to escape but unable to set yourself free. You need holiness to be given freely to you. You need the Liberating King to say over you, "You're free."

That is exactly what he declares over you when you place your trust in him, give over all your strife, and allow him to transform you. There is no condemnation there. No matter how you might sin, he will come to pick you up off the ground and remind you of your true identity. He has declared you free.

I sing the words of the hymn "Before the Throne of God Above" on an almost daily basis. When my enemy, the accuser, comes to me and starts hurling condemnation at me for all the ways I have failed (which are more than I can count), I go back to this song and remember. I fill my mind, memory, and mouth with this incredibly freeing truth.

> When Satan tempts me to despair
> And tells me of the guilt within,
> Upward I look and see him there
> Who made an end of all my sin.
> Because the sinless Savior died
> My sinful soul is counted free.
> For God the just is satisfied
> To look on him and pardon me.[2]

To hear those words coming from my own mouth as I sing the gospel and remind myself that I am not saved by my own holiness, but by Christ's; this is the assurance that frees me to keep pressing on, to keep combating my sin.

I am not holy because I earned it. All my songs and prayers and tears combined couldn't do that for me. I am holy only because I am his.

The one who knew no sin became your sin so that you might become his righteousness. He was broken so that you might be made whole. He bought you with an infinite price. You are not your own. Worship declares Christ's rightful rule and reign over your life and reminds you of the amazing opportunity to honor God with all you are because of all he has done.

You can fight your sin because Jesus is fighting for you. You can have victory in this war because Jesus has already defeated every enemy you face.

Come stand amazed in the splendor of holiness, in the freedom that Christ purchased for you. Let it wash over you.

You are holy because you are his. So come and worship.

Questions for Application and Discussion

1. Are you quick to repent when you sin? Or do you wrestle with justifying your actions? How do you think God thinks about you when you have messed up? Do you believe that your sins are forgiven and you are hidden in Christ?

2. What are your biggest areas of struggle with sin? What lies do you believe that are causing you to struggle in those areas?

3. What would your life look like if every time you were tempted to sin, you replaced those lies with the truth of Scripture and worshiped Christ instead?

10

Hope Not Based on Hype

A FORETASTE OF THE GLORY TO COME

A throne stood in heaven, with one seated on the throne. . . .
Around the throne were twenty-four thrones, and seated on
the thrones were twenty-four elders, clothed in white gar-
ments, with golden crowns on their heads. From the throne
came flashes of lightning, and rumblings and peals of thun-
der. . . . And around the throne, on each side of the throne, are
four living creatures. . . . And day and night they never cease
to say, "Holy, holy, holy, is the Lord God Almighty, who was
and is and is to come!" . . . [The twenty-four elders] cast their
crowns before the throne, saying, "Worthy are you, our Lord
and God, to receive glory and honor and power, for you created all things, and by your will they existed and were created."

Revelation 4:2–11

Then I looked, and I heard around the throne and the living creatures and the elders the voice of many angels, numbering myriads of myriads and thousands of thousands, saying with a loud voice, "Worthy is the Lamb who was slain, to receive power and wealth and wisdom and might and honor and glory and blessing!" And I heard every creature in heaven and on earth and under the earth and in the sea, and all that is in them, saying, "To him who sits on the throne and to the Lamb be blessing and honor and glory and might forever and ever!"

Revelation 5:11–13

A COUPLE OF YEARS BACK, I was leading worship and teaching at a conference for worship leaders from all over the country. On the last night of the conference, as I stood at the back of the room, singing along with six hundred other men and women, I got the sensation that this is what heaven is going to sound like.

Matt Chandler stood in the front row, worshiping and gearing up to preach the last session, but nothing could distract him from bringing everything he had before the God of his salvation. It was impossible to miss his passionate display of adoration; Matt is six feet five with the wingspan of an albatross and he was lifting his hands as high as he possibly could. This image has stayed with me over the years.

What struck me most from that moment was this pastor's heart of worship—he was actually teaching us how to worship, even from the congregation. He was giving us a glimpse of what a heart that was fully enraptured by the love of God could look like, and as he took the platform, he spoke with no less passion.

"You might have a hard time worshiping right now," he said with that deep Matt Chandler rumble in his voice. "But one day, you won't have any problems. When you see God in all his beauty and glory, you're not gonna be able to help yourself from falling on your face and lifting your hands. It's just gonna happen, so get ready."

What a great picture of what it will be like when we finally see the face of the one who gave his life to set us free. No sin to blind us. No brokenness to distract us. It's something to get ready for.

This is how worship frees us for heaven. It is a rehearsal of what is in store, a foretaste of the glory that awaits us.

I have intentionally spent the majority of this book speaking of worship in a rather specific, personalized way. The reason is because I believe we are all always worshiping something or someone and have the amazing opportunity to focus that worship by regularly practicing the presence of God in a variety of ways. So while most of your life of worship will not be a corporate experience, in this final chapter, I really want to focus on the corporate aspects of worship. I believe that nothing prepares us for eternity more than when we gather together to worship as the church.

In corporate worship, God brings his presence down to us. Though heaven is his throne and the earth is his footstool, when we gather to praise and adore him, he meets with us in a special way. As the bride of Christ comes together to meet her Groom and tell of all his wonders, the Holy Spirit fills up that praise and turns it into a pleasing aroma before the throne. Jesus takes us before the Father and we get to be a part of something much, much bigger than ourselves. We get to join in with the song of eternity.

Revelation 4:8 says that all the angels of heaven and the saints who have gone before us *never* stop lavishing praise upon Jesus. Day and night, they are incessantly crying out in thanksgiving for who he is and what he has done! When we worship, we are quite literally joining in with them, singing the song that never ends. I'm not referring to the song you learned as a kid to annoy your friends. No, the only song that will last on into eternity is the same song that we will join the angels and saints in singing: *"Holy, holy, holy, is the Lord God Almighty, who was and is and is to come!"*

The song of eternity is a song of adoration, of praise for the endless worth of the only worthy one! Its first note rang out before time began, as the Father, Son, and Holy Spirit enjoyed one another's presence in an eternal past of unbroken communion and delight. When God created the hosts of heaven, he did not need their praise, but in his loving-kindness and generosity, he created them that they might behold his majesty and complete their enjoyment with worship. The angels began to sing of his holiness and might.

Then came the light, which added brilliant overtones to the song, with day and night each lifting its voice to the Creator. As God called forth the dry land, the trees and mountains and oceans and every kind of animal imaginable each found its harmony and the song began to soar. Then from the dust, God made humankind in his perfect image and gave us lungs to breathe in his life. The Creator began to sing over us, declaring us *very good*, so we joined with all of his creation in response. Our voices became a masterpiece! Every note joining together in concert—a glorious symphony declaring the wonders of our Maker!

Then one day, as Adam and Eve took that first bite of a forbidden fruit, our Master's heart broke and the song took a dark turn. As all of creation fell from the glory it once displayed, its joy-filled shouts of awe and wonder turned to groans of agony, longing to be restored. For thousands of years, we sat in that song, waiting, pining for the hope that God promised in the garden: that one day a Son would come—the Messiah from of old—and his bruised heel would crush the head of the serpent, cursed and cold.

This was the song of the law and the prophets. The song that Israel desperately sang until one night on the hills just outside of Bethlehem, when angels came to a few lowly shepherds and a new song began. The very Son who was foretold had been born. Emmanuel had come to dwell with man. "God with us" had come to save the people from their sin.

For thirty-three years the Lamb of God walked among us and we saw God in the flesh. Every tree, every grain of sand, and every blade of grass, all beholding the promise of restoration coming to pass, hoping to return to the glory they once enjoyed, longing to lift their voices with the same vigor they once had!

But upon a hill that thirty-third year, as the Lamb was led to the slaughter, all of heaven and earth began to feverishly stir. The song grew into a dissonant cacophony as Jesus hung in agony, paying for our sins, bearing the full weight of the penalty we deserved. The earth shook with the thunderous fury of God's relentless love and justice ferociously colliding. Wave upon wave of the wrath that we deserved came crashing down upon the Son of God until he screamed out at the top of his lungs, and with his final breath proclaimed, "It is finished!"

Silence.

All of heaven and earth held its breath waiting for the Savior to rise and lead them once more in the song of the ages. As the sun began to rise that Sunday morning, a voice began to rise with it, growing louder and louder in a crescendo of victory as creation shouted, "He is risen!"

The Lamb was slain to conquer sin once and for all; he had fought death and won. All that was promised was being fulfilled. All that was broken was being healed. All that was lost was being restored. Jesus had risen and was alive once more, never to die again. The Victor had earned the name above every name, so that every knee would bow and every tongue confess that he is Lord. This is the song the saints and angels never stop singing, the song that every tongue will ceaselessly proclaim: *"Worthy is the Lamb who was slain, to receive power and wealth and wisdom and might and honor and glory and blessing!"*

As you and I gather together to worship, we are joining in the wonder and mystery of this great gospel! We are joining with all those gathered around the throne of heaven who are lavishing their adoration upon Jesus. We are preparing ourselves for that moment when we get to heaven and see him for who he is and finally see how everything that he has done from the first to the last was for our good and for his glory.

Imagine the glorious moment of clarity when everything in this life all of a sudden makes sense. A huge grin takes over your face as your soul is overjoyed with a resounding, *"Oh! That's why such and such happened. I never understood, but now I see clearly. God, you really are perfect and wise!"* Worship recognizes this day is coming and shapes your trust here and now in the light of eternity. It causes your hope to become less theoretical and more tangible. Your longing for the things of this world grows weaker as it is replaced with a longing for the one to come—a perfect world filled to overflowing with the glory of God.

God has told us to never stop gathering together to worship and sing about these things in order to remind each other and ourselves that the day is quickly approaching when he will return and make all things right. He knew that we would need that encouragement if we were going to endure to the end.

The sovereign Creator knows everything about the ones he created. He knows you better than you know yourself. When he made you, he knew you would suffer and worry; that temptations would come and you would feel beaten down by the constant battle with sin, pride, and comparison. He knew you would cling to comfort and struggle to love others well, act justly, and live out his mission. He knows that enduring is hard work, and the work never stops.

That is why God gave you corporate worship. To shape you for heaven and free you on earth. To show you the plans he has for you—plans to give you hope and a future. The light at the end of this tunnel is far greater than you can imagine, and worship is the imagining of that light, the anticipation of delighting in its warmth. But it is not an anticipation that will let you down.

If you're anything like me, you have probably fallen victim to the hype machine one too many times. I see a movie trailer that looks amazing, but after shelling out the eighty-four dollars for my movie tickets, I'm depressed that I just wasted two hours of my life and eighty-four dollars that I could have spent on something less terrible. I hear a new restaurant is the best thing my taste buds will ever experience, and I get worked up with the expectation of something that will blow my mind, only to try it and be utterly disappointed. It can be easy to grow increasingly cynical because most things really are too good to be true. Worship is the gift of God to help us combat our cynicism about the hope that is in store for us, a hope that won't disappoint. A hope that's not based on hype.

Every perfect moment when it's difficult to comprehend how life could be any better, every glorious sunset that paints the sky with awe-creating hues, every culinary masterpiece that causes you to roll your eyes back in ecstasy—all of these are foretastes of the glory that is to come, tastes that will pale in comparison to the reality of heaven.

Corporate worship is daring to dream together; to anticipate what true, unending glory will look like; to imagine what it will feel like to be completely enveloped in perfection. It is joining the angels and saints who have tasted and seen for themselves that the Lord is good and who can't stop singing in response. It is getting ready for that moment when we are made whole and holy and we finally see true holiness for the first time. It is kindling a longing for God to fulfill his promises and then pleading with him to do it quickly, singing, "Lord, haste the day when my faith shall be sight!" and "We will wait, for our help is on his way. So come, Lord Jesus!"

God hears our cries. He answers our prayers. And someday soon, as his people are crying out for the freedom of heaven, he will come again. He has promised he will, and he always keeps his promises.

Questions for Application and Discussion

1. Do you long for heaven? Why or why not?

2. It is said that some people are so heavenly minded that they are no earthly good. But those who have done the most for the kingdom of God have likely had the greatest sense of the hope of heaven. How would worshiping in light of the hope of heaven shape the way you live?

3. Take a moment now and imagine a world that is perfect. No pain or sorrow. No sickness or death. Every tear has been wiped away and there is nothing but beauty and bliss for all eternity. This is the promised hope of our perfect Savior. Put this book down and lavish adoration on the God who always keeps his promises.

Notes

Introduction

1. Stephen Miller, "Liberating King," *Liberating King* (Austin, TX: Stephen Miller Ministries, 2015).

Chapter 2 When Sorrows like Sea Billows Roll

1. Horatio G. Spafford, "It Is Well with My Soul," *NetHymnal*, accessed September 29, 2015, http://nethymnal.org/htm/i/t/i/itiswell.htm.

2. Matt Redman, "Never Once," *10,000 Reasons* (Brentwood, TN: Sparrow Records, 2011).

Chapter 6 Moving Beyond Warm Fuzzies

1. John Piper, *Let the Nations Be Glad* (Baker, 1993), 15.

Chapter 9 Ten Looks at Jesus

1. Andrew A. Bonar, *Memoir and Remains of the Rev. Robert Murray M'Cheyne* (London: Hamilton, Adams & Co., 1845), 254.

2. Charitie L. Bancroft, "Before the Throne of God Above," *NetHymnal*, accessed September 29, 2015, http://nethymnal.org/htm/b/e/beforetg.htm.

Stephen Miller is a pastor, artist, songwriter, and a passionate advocate for the local church who travels all over the world to preach and lead worship for various conferences, concerts, camps, and more. He is the president and founder of Rooted Network and lives in Dallas, Texas, with his wife, Amanda, and their five kids.

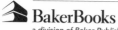